The Collected Edition of The
SPACE VIEWER
1958-1961
Ufo Study Club

BUD KIMES

SAUCERIAN PUBLISHER

ISBN: 9781736731482

© 2021, Saucerian Publisher

Al rights reserved. No part of this publication maybe reproduced, translate, store in a retrieval system, or transmitted in any form or by any means, electronic, mechanical, photocopying, recording or otherwise, without prior written permision from the publisher.

Prologue

It is generally a good idea to return to the classics in any genre. This also goes for UFO literature. Rereading a book after ten or twenty years is a rewarding experience. You will discover new data and ideas you didn´t notice before. The reason, of course, is that you are, in many ways, not the same person reading the book the second or third time. Hopefully you have advanced in knowledge, experience, intellectual and spiritual discernment. A good starting point is to reread the contactee classics of the 1950's, in order to understand the deeper mystery involved in what happened during that era. *SPACEVIEWER* was a saucer mimeographed newsletter published by Bud Kimes, as editor, and F. Park as associate editor under the banner of the U.F.O Study Club of Kansas City, Kansas City, Missouri, , during the late 1950's and early 1960's. The main idea behind *SPACEVIEWER,* like many similar publications of that time, was to create a forum for UFO experience and saucer sightings for the purpose of the investigation of spacecraft, extra-terrestrial travel, and other subjects relating to these matters in order to encourage public support of projects in connection with these phenomena.

Saucerian Publisher was founded with the mission of promoting books in Ufology, Paranormal, and the Occult. Our vision is to preserve the legacy of literary history by reprint editions of books which have already been exhausted or are difficult to obtain. Our goal is to help readers, educators and researchers by bringing back original publications that are difficult to find at reasonable price, while preserving the legacy of universal knowledge. This book is an authentic reproduction of the original printed text in shades of gray. **IMPORTANT:** Despite the fact that we have attempted to accurately maintain the integrity of the original work, the present reproduction may have minor errors beyond our control like: missing and blurred pages, poor pictures and readers' pencil markings from the original scanned copy. Because this book is culturally important, we have made available as part of our commitment to protect, preserve and promote knowledge in the world. These issues are an authentic reproduction of the issues of *SPACEVIEWER* for the years: 1958-1961. Great, but unpretentious, these issues are extraordinarily rare symbols by themselves of what was going on in those early years of the modern UFO era. This collected edition has the following issues of *SPACEVIEWER* : Vol. I, Nos. 3- 5,7-8,9-12 (1958-1959) ;Vol. II, Nos: 1-4,8-10(1959-1960) ;Vol. III, No: 1 (1961).

Editor, Saucerian Publisher, 2021

Bud Kimes, Editor	THE S P A C E V I E W E R	F. Park, Assoc. Ed
Vol. 1 Issue 3	U.F.O. STUDY CLUB Kansas City, Missouri	October 1958

The mailing list has nearly doubled! Over 500 receiving The Space Viewer now! Acquaint friends and neighbors with the purpose of this non-profit organization: Articles of Agreement, Article II, OBJECT: The object of this organization is to assimilate information and to function as a public forum on unidentified flying objects and all that the field embraces.

SUNDAY, OCTOBER 12, 1958, 2:30 p.m., Drexel Hall, Linwood & Baltimore, Kansas City, Mo.

Mr. Otis T. Carr, spaceship designer and inventor of free-energy systems for light and power, OTC Enterprises, Inc., Baltimore, Maryland, will be the speaker for the October meeting of the U.F.O. Study Club!

The introduction alone is terrific, but wait, there's more! A small group of people, your Editor included, had the good fortune to be in the audience of Mr. Carr and Major Wayne S. Aho, Director, Washington Saucer Intelligence, earlier this month here in Kansas City. The gentlemen arrived at 3:00 o'clock in the morning, and in spite of such an unlikely hour, Mr. Carr was bright and voluble for the next two and a half hours about his near future space plans, all of which he will reveal at the public meeting. Included here are a few of the tantalizing highlights.

Mr. Carr has been researching and experimenting for more than twenty years on the principle of free energy and says he has at last tapped the secret and can build a "saucer" which will fly to the Moon. He has set December, 1959, as his date goal for the trip with Major Aho as sole companion passenger. Mr. Carr was asked what he expected to find on the Moon. He replied, "We expect to find bases there established by beings from other worlds." And he facetiously added, "We hope so anyhow. After our two-and-a-half day trip, we'll sure be in a mood for a good hot meal!" Mr. Carr explains why such bases would exist as well as ALL THE INFORMATION HE HAS AVAILABLE as the result of his long labor. HE HOLDS NOTHING SECRET. It is his conviction such information belongs to the people as the only real safety lies in knowing the truth. Further, this is not to be Mr. Carr's first attempt to build a "saucer" type craft. He has already built six test models! Impossible? . . .

Come listen to the man himself! This will be a great day of enlightening information, and as always, the speaker will answer your questions after his talk. Mark your calendars now -- OCTOBER 12.

Donation: Club members, $1.00, and juniors 25¢ (show Club membership card at the door). Non-members, $1.50 and juniors, 12-17, 50¢. Club memberships also available at the door. In all cases of speakers appearing before the U.F.O. Study Club and other such clubs across the country, the speakers leave a greater wealth of information than they take with them in financial gain. Their expenses are heavy and often do well to break even on a lecture tour. Freely we give for that which is being abundantly given to us.

PAST MEETING, September 7, THE MITCHELL SISTERS

The barometer of audience reception has shown this to be one of the best programs yet presented by the Club! And everyone is delighted with Drexel Hall. The Mitchells gave a detailed account of their contacts with space beings and of Helen's ride in a "saucer" and her adventures aboard a "Meired" or mother craft. So fascinating was their talk and answers to questions posed by the interested crowd that it was difficult to close the session. They presented themselves and their talk with utmost sincerity, and the vast fund of knowledge they have acquired concerning space craft and space people was truly astounding. They also tell us they continue to be in regular communication with their space "contacts". It may be possible to present them again at a later date, and with later information. Would you like to hear from them further? Certainly, they are always welcome in our town and in our homes. Incidentally, their mail following their talk here was so voluminous that it took their combined full time for the following week to reply to all the thoughtful folks who wrote.

Such reception also created a demand for copies of their talk. In the interest of satisfying this demand, the Club took the initiative to request permission of Betty and Helen to have the talk mimeographed to distribute at the October 12 meeting only. They graciously consented and 200 copies will be available next meeting at 50¢ per copy. The small margin of net compensation after costs will be turned to the girls as a token of gratitude for this privilege. Again, as was the case in asking them to appear here originally, we called them, they did not call us.

For out-of-towners only: If you will be unable to attend this next meeting and desire a copy of the Mitchell's talk, please mail your request and 50¢ in coin or stamps, and self-addressed, stamped envelope to: Paul M. Wheeler, President of the Club, 1117 Truman Road, Independence, Missouri.

Look for Betty and Helen Mitchell's book, "Among the Saucers", to be published soon. Our best wishes for highest success to these gracious ladies.

SIGHTINGS

Along with the Mitchell sisters came saucer sightings. They, along with other members of your UFO group, were sharing the favorite summer pastime of your Editor--sitting on the back patio. Betty pointed to a light moving northwest overhead. Everyone saw it and observed it turn north in a wide arc and disappear. Again, neither sound nor vapor trail. Paul and Luella Wheeler and Helen M. saw a green flash over the peak of the house. One other fireball type phenomena was seen in the south. Of course, the popular question is, "What did you have to drink?" Well, believe-it-or-not, Ripley, this is a straight coke and iced tea crowd. This was a combination dinner and meeting to arrange for the Club program and later evening appearance on Lee Vogel's Nite Beat. After the evening's activities were concluded, your Editor and his wife were again back on the patio and observed an object at 2:30 a.m. for some 15 minutes. It glowed bright, then dim, then bright again and remained stationary in the sky. This same area in the sky has been checked and rechecked at the same time other nights and only a few dim stars have been seen on clear nights.

Sunday, September 7, 5:30 p.m. (the afternoon of the Mitchell's talk), Mr. Hayes Walker, Jr., at home with his family observed an object appear and travel very fast over his home and then turn north and disappear. He called the Club later to tell of the experience and said the object was much larger in size than the jet aircraft which pass over his house in the area of the Grandview Air Base. He has not previously attended any Club meetings but has been interested in aerial phenomena, reading extensively, and "watching the sky" for nearly two years. He feels patience is rewarded. He further described the object as being round and silvery and silent, traveling at a tremendous rate of speed... NOTE: The Club has received many such calls from persons not connected with the Club since its inception in February, 1957, and many of the calls have been received after the Club meetings. Coincidence? You tell us. Like you, we are trying to fathom it, too. But it might be well to keep all eyes open!

LIBRARY

The Club lending library is progressing with the diligent efforts of its Chairman, Neal Pinkerton. Neal reports some very nice books are coming in, but not quite enough yet to get into business. He receives book donations at meetings, so if you have some to share be sure to bring them. Outside of Club meetings, he will make arrangements to have them picked up. His home phone is JAckson 3-2579, and you can reach him between 7 and 9 in the evening.

THE S P A C E VIEWER   K C Mo 10/58

LIBRARY (Cont)

Lending policies have been worked out as well as many other details and will be duly published just as soon as the library is ready to operate. The Club is contributing extra choice books along with those being donated by individuals. Folks have been waiting a long time for a ready source of reading material on this subject and with your help and push it will be ready to go very soon.

BOOKS

FLYING SAUCER PILGRIMAGE, Helen and Bryant Reeve. Reeve, a graduate engineer of Yale and Massachusetts Institute of Technology, and his wife, due to conflicting information and official denials, decided to make their own investigation. Amazing private research over two years' time and 23,000 miles of travel.

YOU DO TAKE IT WITH YOU, R. DeWitt Miller. This work is the result of Mr. Miller's 25 years psychical research. As well as taking up the "other side" of life, the author says, "What you think affects you, even what you think of flying saucers."

PERIODICALS

PROCEEDINGS, George Van Tassle, Box 419, Yucca Valley, California. Bi-monthly. Van Tassle has been researching in the "saucer" field for 10 years.

FLYING SAUCERS From Other Worlds, Ray Palmer, Box 36, Rt. 2, Amherst, Wisconsin. Bi-Monthly. Sometimes available on the 12th Street newsstands downtown. It has been stated that Palmer is the world's leading New Age publisher.

COSMIC SCIENCE, George Adamski, Star Route, Valley Center, California. Big answers to the big questions about "saucers".

THE LISTENING POST, Clara John, 4811 Illinois Ave., N.W., Washington, D.C. "Comes out when the pot boils over." Chock solid with pointed bits of info.

Repeat:
THE UFO INVESTIGATOR, Major Donald E. Keyhoe, National Investigations Committee on Aerial Phenomena, 1536 Connecticut Ave., Washington 6, D.C. Solid documentary info on UFO's and specialized effort to gain release of officially secret info compiled to date. NICAP, like others in the field, is working against untold hazards, and especially needs our extra support at this time. Help those who are helping us obtain the knowledge we, the people, should have.

ARE YOU A MEMBER OF THE U.F.O. STUDY CLUB?

Memberships to seniors, 18 and over, $2.00 per year; juniors, 12-17, $1.00. Available at Club meetings or by mailing dues to R. E. Kimes, Vice-President/Membership Chairman, 2207 West 79th Terrace, Kansas City 15, Missouri.

A Club membership entitles you to substantial discount on program donation for out of town speakers and ditto for initial deposit for use of the Club library (deposit returned after books returned in event of withdrawal from Club); AND your Club and program news through The SPACE VIEWER each month. This one year ONLY, however, the paid members are generously allowing The Space Viewer to be sent to ALL alike who place their names on the mailing list in order that many more people may become acquainted sooner with the Club. So you non-members who are enjoying this special privilege this year, join and share your interests with the many others in this area.

WHB LISTENERS HEARD "JERRON CRISWELL PREDICTS" ITEM ON SAUCERS

September 2nd, 9:55 and 11:55 p.m. the recorded Criswell prediction broadcast said, "I predict that a new series of sightings will convince America that there is such a thing as a 'flying saucer'. Many authorities who have been silent up to date are speaking out and letting the world know in no uncertain terms that 'flying saucers' do exist. The science fiction stories of yesterday are the facts of today."

THE S P A C E VIEWER   K C Mo 10/58   Page 4

ARE WE BEING WATCHED FROM OUTER SPACE?

The Mitchell sisters say they can do it. Helen tells that aboard the Meired she was taken to a compartment where Alma operated equipment which removed the first vibrations around her home and she saw her mother, her sister, Betty, and their children moving about.

After their stay here in Kansas City, your Editor typed a letter to Helen M., and on rereading the letter, X'd out one paragraph, reset the spacing and X'd it out again. To the naked eye, the contents of that paragraph could not be read. In her reply, Helen TOLD WHAT THE PARAGRAPH HAD SAID!, and commented on the wonder of such mechanical means.

Is our privacy being violated beyond our control? In the above instances and similar goings on reported other places, other times, the evidence would not indicate such abilities being practiced arbitrarily or indiscriminately, but rather constructively and on occasion for illustrative purposes. Hm-m-m, well, just in case it's a Jiminy Cricket "on the shoulder", check what we say to the children, oh, and what we say to Mother, too. Pray for understanding.

See you October 12:   OTIS T. CARR   FLYING SAUCERS ARE FRIENDLY

THE S P A C E VIEWER

Vol. 1, No. 4   U.F.O. STUDY CLUB, KANSAS CITY, MO.   November, 1958

===

| COMING! | COMING! | COMING! |

GEORGE W. VAN TASSLE!

Thursday
November 13th, 1958
8:00 P. M.

DREXEL HALL
Linwood & Main
Kansas City, Mo.

Donation: $1.00 card bearing members; $1.50 others; 50¢ Juniors

BE THERE AND BRING ALL YOUR FRIENDS!   VAN TASSLE HAS A MESSAGE FOR EVERYONE!

It is with great pleasure that your Kansas City Club announces George W. VanTassle, of Giant Rock, California, as our next open forum speaker. He appears for the purpose of bringing his message to EVERYONE. Mr. VanTassle has spent the past ten years of his life in searching out the truths of the Saucer picture. He is the author of two books, "I Rode A Flying Saucer," and "Into This World and Out Again." He also has a large group throughout the world that are working with him in many ways to spread the message he has to offer. He is the publisher of PROCEEDINGS, a monthly paper that carries much valuable information for all persons interested in the Saucer subject. Mr. VanTassle is an ardent researcher and relates his many experiences with both space people and their craft. His information is quite unlimited. He is a capable speaker and has sponsored the Giant Rock Space Convention during the past few years. This man is well worth hearing and is one of the very top in the field. So Come! Tell your friends! Your club is expecting a turnout of record proportions! You are the one who is directly responsible for it! Talk it up AND BE SURE TO COME YOURSELF! Circle that date on your calendar. Make this the most important date of the year up to now. See you there!

INCIDENTALLY: The difference in rates between non-members and others is not to discourage outsiders from coming --- BUT we now have neared the 600 mark for names on our mailing list. This costs the club lots of money. In that our library is costing us quite a sum, and in that this paper costs considerable, we are doing EVERYTHING WE CAN TO INFLUENCE persons to join with us in our association. Halls cost money, speakers have heavy expenses. Postage runs high. We've got expenses. Your share doesn't amount to much. So JOIN WITH US NOW!

OTIS T. CARR: The lecture given by Mr. Otis T. Carr on Sunday, October 12, 1958, was of great interest to all who attended. Mr. Carr had on hand a model of his "saucer" which, he states, operates upon "free energy". He explained that his destination is the moon and the date for such a flight is December, 1959. In an interview with Mr. Carr, it was brought to light that he is now very busy with his project in Baltimore. In fact, he just arrived by auto from Baltimore a few hours before his lecture. His craft has some very fascinating principles, the main one being the wheel within the wheel and the principle that when the counter rotation of these two wheels is in direct ratio with the rotation of the Earth upon its axis, his ship becomes free of gravity and therefore airborne. (Airborne is not the right word for his ship which reacts in the magnetic field which we believe surrounds the Earth and permeates all space.) The interesting thing about this principle is that the same principle is now stated in published and unpublished works on saucers. And Mr. Carr was not conscious of this until AFTER his principles were explained.

INCIDENTALLY: Having heard of Major Wayne S. Aho's marriage to Dorothy Shaeffer, Mr. Carr will either have to build his ship to accommodate another passenger or look for a new one. GOOD LUCK, MAJOR AND MRS. AHO. May good luck be your companion wherever you travel!

SIGHTINGS: Although sightings have been reported, perhaps the most interesting case of this month is given in Newsweek dated October 20, 1958, IN THE FORM OF A DENIAL BY U. S. AIR FORCE OFFICIALS! "Checking It Out," page 34. This item tells of the following incident. Missilemen at a Nike station at Derwood, saw the following: It arrived early in the morning, skittered over the treetops, it landed, casting a weird glow. A three-man team was sent out to check it. What did they find? Nothing on the ground. Their conclusions: A falling star or meteorite had been sighted and a 200 watt bulb in a farmer's barnyard caused the glow. Now let's just look at this for a moment. Who saw it? Nike missilemen who, we understand, are highly trained technicians and in all probability observers. If they don't know a light skittering across the treetops from a falling meteorite, then you better not throw your hat up at the next football game you go to -- or you might end up with a nike missile through it! So we add these observers to the long list of Air Force pilots, the radar men, the Ground Observers, Patrolmen, Policemen, etc., who don't know what they are seeing. What was the weird glow? A two hundred watt lamp on a farmer's barn. Having a few hay seeds in my own hair and quite a few callouses from shucking corn, I always found there was no friendlier light than a farmer's barnyard light and during all the years spent in the farming country, never once did one cast a weird glow. Maybe that's because hardly anyone goes through a night without seeing quite a number of them and can recognize them immediately for what they are. The ending of the article didn't sound as if the writer or editor was buying it very thoroughly. Thanks to Newsweek for this excellent report.

FRONT PAGE NEWS: Almost everywhere one looks nowadays one sees the Air Force reports that all but two per cent of the reportings have been explained. It is not the intent or policy of this paper or this organization to try in any way to discredit our U.S. Air Force, for they are a fine organization and everyone is proud to see any one of our young men, straight and tall in his blue uniform sporting wings. It brings to all a sense of confidence and pride in the services and the youth of this great country. Yet, the Air Force does adopt a policy every once in a while that is quite hard to fathom. Perhaps they have a very good reason for their attitude and we give them full credit for it and do not want to question it. However, we also have a responsibility upon our shoulders to try and get as much pertinent information as we can to those who wish to judge for themselves. Questioning and thinking is the inherent right that our forefathers fought and died for, that we might have it in full. Let's use that right and practice it! Make your own decisions, and don't let ANYONE ELSE DO IT FOR YOU! Two weeks ago, one local paper published on its front page such a report. Your editor wrote the editor of that paper and here is the jist of that letter, which, incidentally wasn't published:

"In regard to the report that the U.S.Air Force has said that all but two per cent of all flying object reports have been accounted for: During World War II this writer was on Wake Island and was captured there and remained there as a prisoner of the Japanese for ten months and then was sent on to Japan. During that period, we prisoners had hidden a radio in one of the brushy areas of this island and in that way had access to all the island during the entire day, used this radio to tune in news broadcasts from Honolulu. We were amazed at what was broadcast about attacks on Wake Island when attacked by Allied Planes and Forces was almost opposite to what had actually happened during those attacks, and personally observed by ourselves." Nuf sed.

BOARD MEETING: It is at the request of your board that ALL members of the U.F.O. Study Club be invited to attend these meeting. We are in need of much help. The job of Treasurer is open, plus the job of program chairman. We need help to keep things going the way you want them to go. Executive Board meetings are held on the third Sunday of every month at the Kansas City Museum in north section of the city. Plan to come! Call either Mrs. Bennett at WA 1-8170 or Paul Wheeler at CL 2-3351 for exact time and date. Come. We need your help and advice. We are planning to get together where we can talk more closely with each other and present for your inspection literature, a list of books in file at the library, and a list of tapes available either for copying or free playing before your group. Let's hear from you regarding these matters. Box 412, Kansas City 41, Mo., is our address. Use our box. Let's hear from you.

It is with great regret that the Board accepted the resignation of Mrs. Francie Park from all duties connected with our club. Her reasons are worthy and although all members hated to see her leave, her resignation was reluctantly accepted. Her help has been most invaluable, to say the least, and all members hold the very highest regard for Mrs. Park and her abilities. We hope it will not be too long before she can return and take up her responsibilities again. Her message to all is:

"Personal Greetings: Hello to all you good UFO'ers and friends. Fellowship in this field is the most wonderful opportunity to meet the most WONDERFUL people in the world! Alas, the demand of personal affairs now precludes my continuing in office or as assoc. editor, so I must formally resign all official duties, but will retain Club membership and active interest. There are many of you who have much to give this effort, but have been somewhat shy about coming forward, since we are all very widespread and have not had proper social contact. Let this be an appeal to you to take the initiative to take part. The too few working members of the Club need you and welcome you! And you know your rewards are always greater than the efforts expended. Will be seeing you regularly at Club meetings and will always be glad to hear from you. (Am in the phone book.) Much success and warmest wishes to the Executive Board members, Club members and friends. Francie Park, past Vice Pres./Program Chm. 10-26-58."

Good luck, Francie! We know you're near -- just in case.

STORY OF THE WEEK: A friend called the other day and told a little story that might be of interest. The person of whom she spoke had just gotten a flash from inside sources that the "saucers were flying". The time was around eleven o'clock at night. Mr. Eager Beaver (the boy that had received the message) immediately dug out the old army cot, got out a few heavy blankets, brewed a canteen of coffee and made a bed under the stars. He wanted to be in on the show. No sooner had he hit the bed than--Blooey! -- You guessed it. He went to sleep. Don't YOU sleep through the big show! Keep awake! Keep your lamps trimmed and full of oil!

HERE'S ORIGINALITY: The following poem was just received by President Paul M. Wheeler from one of our ardent members, Mrs. Julia T. Brogan. We appreciate her inspiration and are glad to share it with our readers:

U F O ' S

Oh shining discs in heaven's deepening blue,
   As silently you scan our infant world,
What hopes, what dreams, transmit to earth through you--
   Protected, shielded--as through space you whirled?

From what far planet comes your lovely sign?
   What destiny--infinity--you merge?
The galaxies roll on, complete, divine.
   Earthbound, wild wars and tumult round us surge.

Are you our guide to deeper, richer life?
   Our brothers, who this earth have often trod?
Teach us your ways--tranquility for strife--
   Help us to know we serve a mutual God.

                --Mrs. Julia T. Brogan
                3003 Independence Avenue
                Kansas City 24, Mo.

PARTING THOUGHT:

"He must increase, but I must decrease. He that cometh from above is above all; he that is of the earth is earthly, and speaketh of the earth: He that cometh from heaven is above all." -- John 3:30-31.

Let's all just kinda keep our thoughts and eyes in that direction, what say?

AND WHO'S WHO FOR DECEMBER? -- Well that IS a SURPRISE!

COMING!   COMING!   COMING!   COMING!   COMING!   COMING!

WHEN?   WHO?   VAN TASSLE, THAT'S WHO!   WHERE?

November 13, 1958
8:00 p.m.

Drexel Hall
Linwood & Main
Kansas City, Mo.

UFO STUDY CLUB
KANSAS CITY

THE SPACE VIEWER

Vol. 1, No. 5   U.F.O. Study Club, Kansas City, Mo.   December, 1958

==

| COMING! | HE'LL BE HERE NOVEMBER 30, SUNDAY, AT DREXEL HALL | COMING! |

GEORGE ADAMSKI!!!!

| EVERYONE COME! | SUNDAY, NOVEMBER 30, 1958 | BRING A FRIEND! |
| USE YOUR PHONE | DONATION ADMISSION $1.50 FOR EVERYONE | INVITE SOMEONE |

==

ADAMSKI TO GIVE LECTURE TO UFO STUDY CLUB: On November 30, Sunday, at Drexel Hall, George Adamski, author of two of the most famous books on UFO'S and space people, will speak before the UFO Study Club at Drexel Hall.

Mr. Adamski was the first to receive world wide recognition when he announced that he had contacted beings from other planets and had been aboard their ships. Mr. Adamski, in his works, describes his first contact with the beings and the unique way in which they presented themselves. His book states that he was taken up in one of their Scout-Craft and was taken to a mother ship hovering far above the Earth's surface.

In a later trip he was taken near the moon and could see it's surface quite clearly. He also was taken near to the surface of the planet Venus and saw much activity on this planet. Although others now claim to have made similar trips, Mr. Adamski's adventures were the first to receive world wide publication.

Mr. Adamski, in his years of Saucer research, has taken many interesting photographs of operational craft. Mr. Adamski has much to offer all those interested in any way with Saucer phenomena. Call your friends! Meet with us at Drexel Hall, Baltimore and Linwood. Donation fee, EVERYONE, $1.50. Sunday, November 30, 2:30 P.M.

GEORGE VANTASSEL: Mr. George W. VanTassel gave a very interesting and worth while talk before the UFO Study Club on November 13th. He told of the work being carried on at his place in Yucca Valley, California.

SPECIAL INTEREST

INFORMAL GET-TOGETHER----CLUB MEMBERS AND THEIR FRIENDS----December 14, 2:30 P.M. At the Kansas City Museum, 3218 Gladstone Blvd., in the dining hall, at 2:30 P.M. Mrs. Dellaverne Owen will bring us a short Christmas message. Refreshments and a get-acquainted hour will follow. If you have books to donate to the library, please bring them.

TAPE RECORDINGS

Members with tape recorders are urged to take advantage of club tape recording services. Complete lists of available tape recordings, collected from all over the country and including most of the personalities in the UFO field, are ready for distribution to members upon request. The club's tape recording committee is set up to make copies of recordings for those who want them, provided blank tape is furnished to make the copies on.

For those groups who would like to hear certain recordings, but do not have access to a recorder, arrangements can be made for someone to bring a recorder to play tapes.

To obtain a tape list and for additional information, please contact Charles Bennett, 2632 Cypress Ave., Kansas City, Mo., Phone, WA 1-8170. Or Dwight Brockman, 10915 W. 57th Terrace, Shawnee, Kansas, Phone, HE 2-7743. Tape lists can also be obtained at any club meeting.

First Vice President Appointed

Mr. Dwight Brockman, 10915 W. 57th Terrace, Shawnee, Kansas, has been named as First Vice President, Executive Chairman of the program committee, by the Executive Board, to fill the vacancy left by the resignation of Mrs. Francie Park.

Mel Bez De Son   Peace Be With You

DON'T FORGET ADAMSKI!   BRING YOU FRIENDS!   DREXEL HALL -- NOVEMBER 30th, 2:30 PM.
---1

Vol. 1, No. 7   T H E S P A C E V I E W E R   Dwight Bockman,
January, 1959   U.F.O. Study Club, Kansas City, Mo.   Editor.

It was from a little acorn that the oak tree grew.

2ND ENGAGEMENT FOR MITCHELL SISTERS: Betty and Helen Mitchell are scheduled for another saucer lecture at Drexel Hall, Linwood and Baltimore, January 11, 2:30 p.m.

These young ladies are from Florissant, Missouri, a suburb of St. Louis. Both are mothers, Helen having a daughter, and Betty a daughter and two sons. They were born in Carthage, Missouri, and moved to St. Louis with their parents at an early age where they received their schooling.

In September they spoke for us, stating many things of a scientific nature. They told of contact with space people and of Helen's trip into space where she visited a mother craft.

We understand they have all new material for their return engagement, much of which they have received since September. Their first contact was in May, 1957, and they are still communicating with these people from Mars.

We recall a well pleased audience in September. We expect a well pleased audience January 11.

As usual, the expenses have to be paid so we ask a donation of $1.00, or 50¢ for the juniors, 12 through 17.

CLIPPER GEMS

From Baltimore, Md., Sun., Oct. 27, 1958 -- Phillip Small and Alvin Cohen reported two UFO over a bridge at Loch Raven Reservoir last night as they were driving along Loch Raven Road. They reported seeing a round, white, egg-shaped object floating or suspended over Bridge No. 1. They said the object appeared to be about 100 feet long. As they approached to within 75 feet of the bridge the motor of their car and all the electricity went off. They got out of the car and observed this object for about 45 seconds to one minute, after which the object glowed very intensely and threw off a lot of heat. The object then shot straight up in the air with a loud clap or the sound of an explosion. The object then disappeared within five or ten seconds. Small said after he got back in his car the motor started immediately and the lights turned on. He also stated the heat was so intense he believed his cheek on the left side was burned.

From Frederick, Md., News, Oct. 20, 1958 -- Allen Etzler, 26-year-old cabinet maker and former radar operator of Laytonsville, said he was driving home from work about 9:30 one night when he glanced off to one side of the road and saw what looked like a "glowing ball". When first sighted, he said, it was only "about as high as a silo", but within a few seconds shot upward into the night at a startling speed. It was soon out of sight overhead. His story of the "glowing ball" comes shortly after several other residents of this section of the state had reported a bright flaring light in the sky.

From Garden Grove, Calif., Daily News, October 23, 1958 -- Richard H. Osterloh, 34, of Anaheim, Calif., said he saw a UFO over Disneyland. "It was the size and shape of a blimp, surrounded by a halo glow and with three or four brightly shining colored lights in the center. It had a tail about three or four times the length of the object itself, with a bright light shining at the end. It was about 12:30 a.m. when I first saw it. I was driving home from work. It seemed to be about 300 yards over Disneyland parking lot. I drove along slowly and watched it for about two minutes. Then it took a sharp dive and disappeared in a bright flash as it neared the ground.

A UFO photograph taken by a youth in the same area last year aroused considerable interest throughout the nation and was picked up by investigators from the U.S. Air Force for study.-- Thanks to Dr. Buehli.

DOCUMENTATION SUGGESTED

Many reports of UFOs in our local area have been voiced, time and time again, only to be lost in the shuffle. Charles Bennett, of 2632 Cypress, suggests that we try to accumulate these sightings and make them a matter of record. If you will call Charles at WA 1-8170, or Dwight Bockman at HE 2-7743. They will arrange to put your statement on tape, or if you prefer, write it in to the Spaceviewer. Send your material to Dwight L. Bockman, 10915 West 57th Terrace, Shawnee, Kansas.

LIFE ELSEWHERE IN THE UNIVERSE?

From New York Times, November 16, 1958. Dr. Melvin Calvin, University of California chemist known for his pioneering studies of the chemical processes of photosynthesis, stated in a lecture at the University of Washington last week that "given the original physical conditions of the primordial earth, the genesis and evolution of life, including complex forms like man, have followed virtually an inevitable pattern".

Dr. Calvin based his reasoning upon knowledge that has been built up in recent years in many chemical laboratories, including his own, about the primordial earth and its atmosphere and the subsequent evolution of inorganic into organic (carbon-containing) molecules of growing complexity, which led to the development of structures having the characteristic of life.

Predictable pattern: Chemical knowledge, Dr. Calvin said, is now great enough to propose with some certainty that the evolution of chemicals up to and including a living cell occurred in a predictable and inevitable pattern. With higher forms than the cell, however, determinism prevailed under broader conditions. Thus, he said, it could be expected that plants and animals would develop, but that their precise form would not be predetermined.

Observational scientific evidence, he added, suggests the existence of life--including plants and animals-- widely throughout the universe. The plants and animals might not look like those on earth. But having a comparable environment, they would have similar sense organs, such as seeing and hearing organs. There would, in Dr. Calvin's view, be living forms--capable, like man, of thought.

An implication of such a concept, he said, is that life is a major cosmic phenomenon, rather than a trivial accident on an insignificant planet, and that thinking creatures may be altering their environment throughout the universe even more profoundly than man has altered the earth.

As man launches his machines and himself into space, he continues, he will transform other planets in the same way that he transformed the surface of the earth.

Man's venture into space, he concluded, is not a mere demonstration of his strength; it is an inevitable and necessary aspect of evolution, which depends upon each organism's developing its every potential to the greatest extent.
--Thanks Mr. Pinkerton.

NEW APPOINTMENTS

Mr. Dwight Bockman, 1st Vice-President, was named editor of the Spaceviewer by the Executive Board at their last meeting. Mr. Robert C. Moran, Rt. 3, Box 444, Independence, Mo., has been named 2nd Vice-President and Chairman of the Membership Committee, by the board to fill the vacancy left by the resignation of Bud Kimes. A finance committee was created to study the club's financial needs, establish admission fees, etc. This committee consists of Mr. Derrick Bennett, Mr. Charles Caspari, and Mr. Neal Pinkerton.

ADAMSKI STAY ENJOYED

The UFO Study Club of Kansas City thoroughly enjoyed the lecture given by Mr. George Adamski on November 30. Open house at the home of President Paul M. Wheeler for Mr. Adamski and his secretary, Mrs. Lucy McGinnis, was enjoyed by the executives of the club and friends of our guests. Over 40 people came and participated in a covered dish supper in the evening. All testified to a most profitable time. We all regretted to see Mr. Adamski and Mrs. McGinnis leave after their work was done here. They are truly endeared in the hearts of all of us and we shall long remember the valuable information and advice they have brought to us. May God go with you where ere you go - George and Lucy.

CLUB SOCIAL HIGHLIGHTS

Thirty eight members attended the social get-together Sunday, December 14. This occasion provided a common ground on which friendships were more closely knit together.

Two very enlightening highlights of the afternoon were talks made by Charles Caspari and Paul Wheeler.

Mr. Caspari gave the club a condensed translation of a German metaphysical paper. The name of the publication he translated as "The New Europe". It told of landings on German territory. It stated that the planet Venus had much representation in Santiago, Chili. Another very interested translation was that the community heads of Venus have decided to effect a landing here on earth and that they have chosen the German territory.

Mr. Wheeler pointed out a recent article in the Kansas City Star about a possible new means of financing other than the monetary system. He pointed out that this had previously been given the Mitchell sisters as a prediction. He stated that we need to keep our minds open to the things that go on around us in this fast moving age. Mr. Wheeler told the club of a sighting he had back about the time the Wright Brothers were first getting off of the ground. He said it was about the size of a full moon at its largest, as it looks when it has just come up over the horizon. He reported it came low over the tree tops and he could see the tree tops waver. It went across the sky at a rapid pace. Mr. Wheeler pointed out also in his talk that he was informed by Mr. Wayne Aho that a Congressman had been contacted, and the Air Force interviewed him for hours getting the information which he had to give pertaining to that contact.

Plenty of refreshments were made available by the ladies. Cookies were in many sizes and colors. Were the little green ones supposed to be for the "little green men"?

This affair took place in the basement of the Kansas City Museum. This small banquet room has an excellent kitchen facility attached and provides a fine meeting place for smaller crowds.

LIST OF SAUCER CLUBS BEING COMPILED

Frances Bennett, club secretary, is compiling a list of flying saucer clubs. She now has 85, which includes organizations in 20 states, Hawaii, Argentina, Australia, Brazil, Canada, England, France, New Zealand, Japan, South Africa, Switzerland. This list will be posted at the meetings for additions or corrections. This will be a handy list to take on your vacation.

CLUB LIBRARY IN OPERATION

The UFO Library is open for business. It requires a deposit of $1.00 for members, or $2.50 for non members. The Club pays the postage one way and the borrower pays return postage. You may keep the books four weeks, after that a 4 cents per day fine is levied. Mail your deposit to Mr. Neal Pinkerton, Box 412, Kansas City 41, Missouri.

Vol. 1, No. 8 THE SPACEVIEWER Dwight Bockman,
February, 1959 U.F.O. Study Club, Kansas City, Mo. Editor.

Truth is the only thing that changes not. Page 48, Aquarian Gospel.

DAN MARTIN SPEAKS FEBRUARY 8: Dan M. Martin, a 60-year-old Detroit man, will tell the UFO Study Club of his experiences with space craft. The lecture, as usual, will be at Drexel Hall, Linwood and Baltimore, 2:30 p.m. Sunday, February 8.

For more than 20 years Mr. Martin has been receiving what he terms "unorthodox information". He was born and raised in a small town in Texas which no longer exists. It was only in recent months that Mr. Martin made his home in Detroit.

Due to the things he told, Mr. Martin's family and friends turned against him. His property and money were taken from him and he was directed to go into Mexico where he continued his study.

Mr. Martin stated his first contact with a space craft was in August, 1955, at which time he was told he would be contacted again. He was contacted again June 11, 1956. At this time he was taken aboard a large space ship. He spent approximately seven hours as their guest, and attended a lecture by the master of the ship.

He said in a letter to the club, "I heard and saw many things of interest, and I shall be glad to tell these things just as I saw and heard them. What I saw and heard has caused me personally to completely readjust my mode of living and thinking. I am not a preacher nor a religious fanatic in any way, since I do not belong to any religious group. I'll simply tell it as it was told to me."

He has written three books, "The Watcher," "Seven Hours Aboard A Space Ship," and "Seal of Daniel Broken."

We urge you to bring a friend to this lecture. Fill your car up with the people around you. This is a thriving, growing club. Let's keep it growing. Donations will be $1.50 for adults, 50 cents for juniors 12 through 17.

K. C. STAR GIVES SPACE MAPS

With the compliments of "This Week" magazine which is soon to be a part of the Sunday Star, the club received five copies of an excellent space map, printed in color, and an accompanying booklet of explanation called Key Guide to Outer Space. We express our appreciation to The Star for this fine piece of workmanship.

OF SCIENTIFIC INTEREST

Some interesting articles have been appearing in the news lately that seem to have a familiar ring to them.

In the January 6 Kansas City Times appeared an article by Arthur J. Snider, Chicago Daily News science writer, about a new refrigeration and heating principle. It is thermoelectricity.

The article said the principle of thermoelectricity has been known for many years, but the efficient materials to permit its practical application are only now being discovered.

The new development is founded on the knowledge that when two dissimilar metals, known as semiconductors, are joined end to end and heated, they will generate an electric current.

If a drop of water is placed on the junction and the current made to flow in one direction, the water will freeze. When the current direction is reversed the ice will melt. Thus the junction liberates heat in one case and absorbs heat in the other.

Listed among the merits of the principle was "keep cold foods cold on dinner plates and hot foods hot."

This item has a familiar sound. At the Buck Nelson convention last June, Lee Childers, a Detroit baker, spoke. Among other experiences he related eating in a dining hall on the moon, and told of a rotating table on which hot foods were kept hot, frigid foods kept frigid, and vegetables that need a drink were kept in proper condition.

Its interesting to note comparisons as we look through the news. Where do we go from here? Utopia next stop?

Another interesting item of the news, though a little bit old, comes from the December 13 Times. Bearing an Oklahoma City dateline of December 12, it states that Otis T. Carr, president of O. T. C. Enterprises, Inc., Baltimore, Md., filed an application for a license to pilot a space craft with the Civil Aeronautics Administration at Oklahoma City.

Those who heard Mr. Carr speak here a few months ago will recall he stated he intended to build a space craft and make a trip to the moon in December of this year.

Speaking of inventors, here is an interesting little paragraph. In Los Angeles a self-educated inventor who has a device to prevent plane collisions finally is found in a hobo camp where he had fled because he couldn't sell his idea. Now the government will spend 5 million dollars developing the invention. Which shows -- patience always pays, even if you don't have it.

FUSION!

"I am an Englishman . . ." "And I an American--"
"And I'm of Italian birth."
(But some day the natives of Mars will say---
"So--you are from the Earth!")

SISTER TEAM PROVIDES VARIETY IN LECTURE

Helen and Betty Mitchell of Florissant, Missouri, gave the club a different kind of lecture January 11. They gave an extensive report of a tremendous city on Mars called Vrss.

Using a group of colored diagrams which they had drawn, Betty and Helen showed how the city was arranged with the palace and palace grounds in the center. They told of the residential sections and industrial sections surrounding the palace grounds. They talked at some length about the government installations on Mars. Seems there is one section of 12 buildings where each planet of the solar system has a representation. One building is for earth, and it seems to be without representation.

At the end of their lecture was a message they brought from the space people especially for us as follows:

"Peace be with you, beloved. In the light of mind evolveness one chooses to serve, and in so doing turns the forces of love in this attraction towards him. When searching is difficult it proves advancement, for adversaries must work strongly to prevent evolvement. Let darkness fade to the nothingness it is, not potential or manifesting as is the light which takes its place. Peace be with you."

Their lecture in mimeographed form will soon be available through the UFO Club at 50¢ each. Address Mr. Paul Wheeler, 1117 W. Truman Rd., Independence, Mo.

CLAIMS U. S. HAS CAPTURED FLYING SAUCER

(This article comes to us without dateline and without source. We have no means of checking on it, but give it to you for what it may be worth.)

By John Lester

The United States Air Force has captured at least one and possibly two flying saucers--unidentified flying objects from outer space--A top Washington official said yesterday.

It also is "believed on excellent authority" that France has at least two, England one, Russia one, "and there's a distinct possibility" the Brazilian air force has another.

The highly placed Washington source, who refused to be identified, said a rumor to the effect that the USAF has a saucer "stashed away at a secret base has persisted for quite some time but no one has been able to confirm or run it down as far as I know." However, the fact that the Air Force is known to have designed its own saucer-type craft according to flying saucer specifications "lends definite credence to the rumor," the source states. It would be "virtually impossible," he pointed out, for the Air Force to duplicate such a craft unless "it had one in its possession."

The Air Force saucer, he said, has been undergoing "tests and experiments" at the Wright Patterson Base at Dayton, Ohio, but to date it hasn't been able to come anywhere near the high speeds and fantastic maneuverability of unidentified flying objects (UFO) sighted by competent pilots and others and tracked by skilled government radar men thousands of times.

Further credence is given the rumor, the source said, by the Air Force's "original anxiety" to "get a UFO by any possible means." Military pilots, he says, were ordered to accomplish this by shooting one down or, if necessary, "even ramming it and bailing out."

Added to this, it was pointed out, are public statements by William Lear, a world authority on aerodynamics and winner in 1950 of the coveted Collier Trophy for outstanding contributions to aviation. The Collier Award was presented by President Truman. In these statements, carried by the wire services several months ago, Lear disclosed this country soon will be turning out saucer-type craft that eventually will attain speeds up to 10,000 miles an hour.

Authority for the report that England has a flying saucer is Lord Louis Montbatten. No one willing or able to be quoted on, reports France, Brazil and Russia also have flying saucers in their possession could be reached, although a wire service story from London yesterday stated the Soviet plan to build a jet-powered saucer in the near future. The Soviets have admitted, the story stated, that in recent tests a model of the planned craft has proved "extremely maneuverable."

It was also learned yesterday of the existence of a special Senate sub-committee (as yet unnamed) and two Congressional committees, one of which is working on space legislation and related matters, all formed for the purpose of investigating "The UFO Problem" from every conceivable angle. The Senate group, headed by Sen. John N. McClellan, (D-Ark.), has had the matter under study the past 18 months.

It is expected this committee will go into action after a powerful congressional body, just after the first of the year, launches a study of the government's guided missiles program.

Word is the latter investigation has been sparked by a feud between Wernher Von Braun, the scientist heading the program, and Secretary of Defense Neil McElroy over certain delays in the schedule of firings and the "general confusion" that has surrounded the United States missiles program from the beginning.

UFO INVESTIGATIONS BUREAU

UFO Investigations Bureau Civilian Intelligence, David A. Lopez, director, 2107 Bancroft Street, Saginaw, Michigan, was organized as an investigating agency to obtain accurate information from responsible sources and to determine and ascertain authentic sighting reports. Anyone desiring to give IBCI information may write for report blanks. Membership fees are $3.00 per year.

LIBRARY NEWS

The club librarian, Mr. Neal Pinkerton, had a fine display of the UFO library set up on the balcony at the last meeting. A number of people went up to see the display and check out books. He intends to make that his regular stand of business during the meetings. Mr. Pinkerton will be glad to help you with your reading problems and to advise you on different phases of reading, so go on up the stairs and call on him at our next meeting.

Incidentally, the club is still in need of many books. If you have UFO books to donate, or if you have funds to donate for new books please contact Mr. Neal Pinkerton, JA 3-2579.

It is expected that Mr. Martin, our February speaker, will bring a supply of his books and can be purchased at the meeting. If there are other UFO books you wish to order please contact Mr. Pinkerton and order them through the Club.

Vol. 1, No. 9   T H E S P A C E V I E W E R   Dwight Bockman,
March, 1959   U.F.O. Study Club, Kansas City, Mo.   Editor

PROFESSIONAL MAN SCHEDULED FOR MARCH

Dr. Wallace C. Halsey, D.D., L.L.D., professional engineer, scholar and minister, president of Christ Brotherhood, Inc., of Joshua Tree, California, is scheduled to speak Sunday, March 8, 2:30 p.m., at Drexel Hall, Linwood and Baltimore.

Dr. Halsey has had many interesting experiences and speaks on a very wide range of subjects, including the role of spaceships, the story of creation, our solar system and balance, the Star of David, the Tower of Babel, the twelve planets of our solar system, functions of the pyramids, the California pyramid, infinite light, positive and negative light, "squaring" the body, the pineal gland, third eye development, spaceships and space people, life on Saturn, the center of earth, effects of the destruction of the planet Lucifer, the unnatural crust on the surface of the earth, differences in the structure of spaceships of Mars, Venus and Saturn, the transistor beam and others.

Of course Dr. Halsey will not be able to cover every one of these subjects, but the question and answer period will provide an opportunity to gain information on the subject you desire. The public address system is getting some attention and it is expected that both microphones will be operating in good order.

The speaker will be able only to touch the surface of the many phases involved, but being a man of much formal education and much experience, we are assured of a very informative lecture.

The donation will be $1.50 for nonmembers, $1.00 for members, 50 cents for juniors, 12 through 17.

Fill your car up with your neighbors, and if you have lots of neighbors make an extra trip. The club needs your support and you need the club.

The organization has weathered the storms over the past year and a half and has reached a footing of solid ground. It is rapidly gaining recognition throughout the country. We feel it is already among the best of them. It is because of your support. It will be because of your support that it goes on to spread greater light in days ahead.

UNEXPLAINED TREMORS IN SEPARATED AREAS

The Texas Panhandle and Southeastern New Mexico were rocked by a tremor Feb. 10. Flagstaff, Arizona, was shaken by a mysterious jolt the morning of Feb. 11. On Feb. 12 mysterious rumbling blasts shook three Pacific Northwest cities at separate intervals about two hours apart. Seattle at 5:38 p.m.; Oregon City, Ore., at 7:28 p.m.; and Yakima, Wash., at 9:15 p.m.

Several persons in Seattle reported seeing a "red streak falling slowly into Puget Sound."

Houses shook and dishes rattled in all of the areas, but the strangest phenomena occurred in the Flagstaff area and the West Texas-New Mexico area.

In Flagstaff, drivers on their way to work said immediately after the tremor their windshields were iced over both inside and outside. The Associated Press teletype machine at the Arizona Daily Sun went on the blink, then returned to normal service a few minutes later.

The Texas tremor, accompanied by two distinctive blasts, shook an area from 100 miles northeast of Amarillo to Roswell, New Mexico, 200 miles southwest. Witnesses said houses swayed and they reported hearing unpleasant noises like trucks hitting buildings, horses galloping and gas explosions.

FALLOUT FOUND IN WHEAT

St. Paul, Minn.--Minnesota scientists have turned up a batch of northern plains wheat, grown between 1956 and 1958, that contained more than six times the supposed tolerable limit of strontium-90 produced by nuclear fallout.

The batch was one of 30 sampled from 10 areas over a 3-year period. The scientists said the strontium-90 average of all 1958 wheat crop samplings was $1\frac{1}{2}$ times the "safe limit" set forth by the Atomic Energy Commission. In contrast, the 1956 crop was barely over the limit.

Disclosure of the strontium-90 results was made by a Minnesota commission appointed by Gov. Orville Freeman to probe crop radio-activity over the 3-year period beginning in 1956.

"We did not expect to find as high quotas in the wheat as we did," commission spokesman Dr. Maurice B. Vissher, chief of the University of Minnesota medical schools psysiology department, said.

"The situation undoubtedly will get worse if the world continues nuclear bomb testing," he said.

STAMPS IT, BUT NOT TOP SECRET

Mr. Henry Kramkowski, of Hamilton, Ontario, Canada, head of the Canadian branch of the Aetherius Society of England, has an interesting way of stating his thought about radiation. He stamps each envelope he mails out with a rubber stamp. It reads: "Better be ACTIVE today than RADIOACTIVE tomorrow. Ban the Bomb Tests NOW."

QUOTE OF THE MONTH

From Fate Magazine, March, 1959, issue--"I believe that 'flying saucers' are piloted by supernatural forms of life who have observed earth for a long time. I call these creatures Unaniden and believe they are very intelligent beings."--Prof. Hermann Oberth, father of modern rocketry.

THOUGHT OF SPACE

My studies of the outer space
   Make it clear to see
That it's what fills the "inner space"
   That means the most to me. -- Florence Maltby.

THE GENERAL SHOULD LISTEN

Washington--The Army's director of special weapons told an inquiring House committee today he does not believe in flying saucers; but he added a strong qualification. "I speak in fear and trepidation," said Maj. Gen. William W. Dick, Jr., "because my wife believes they exist."

PRIVATE GROUP SPONSORS HUGH LYNN CAYCE

Hugh Lynn Cayce of Virginia Beach, Virginia, will be in Kansas City March 26, and will speak that evening at Drexel Hall, 8:00 p.m. Admission donation $1.00. Hugh Lynn Cayce is the son of Edgar Cayce, one of the truly remarkable psychics of all times. A number of books have been written about Edgar Cayce, among which are, "There Is A River," by Thomas Sugrue; "The World Within" and "Many Mansions," by Dr. Gina Cerminara.

ARTICLE IDENTIFIED

The article printed in our February Spaceviewer entitled "Claims U. S. Has Captured Flying Saucer" has been identified by the contributor, Larry Lindvig of Chicago, midwest director of Tape Recorded UFO Information Service, as being from the Jersey Journal, Jersey City, N. J., Dec. 22, 1958.--Thanks, Larry.

MARTIN BRINGS FRIENDS

The Dan Martin lecture in February enjoyed a good attendance. Many people lingered on after the lecture and gathered around the platform to ask further questions of Mr. Martin. A delightful surprise was Al and Ruth Korinek, who accompanied Dan from Detroit. Al gave a talk before the lecture, and on Saturday evening showed a group of UFO slides. Al and Ruth have received communication in their own right. These two are lights along the way and their light is for all who wish to share.

WHERE TO FIND PEACE

From This Week Magazine, February 22--In this era of world wars, in this atomic age, values have changed. We have learned that we are the guests of existence, travelers between two stations. We must discover security within ourselves. (Cont.)

During our short span of life we must find our own insights into our relationship with the existence in which we participate so briefly. Otherwise, we cannot live!

This means, as I see it, a departure from the materialistic view of the nineteenth century.

It means a reawakening of the spiritual world, of our inner life--of religion. I don't mean religion as a dogma or as a church, but as a vital feeling.

These words were spoken by a brave non-Communist citizen of Soviet Russia, Boris Pasternak.

TV PROGRAM PROVES SKEPTICISM DOESN'T PAY

Mr. Bill Robe, a contestant on People Are Funny (6:30 p.m., Sat., Feb. 21) learned too late the folly of unreasoning skepticism. Dan Fry, Calvin Girvin, and Gabriel Green appeared on the program to try to convince the typical disbeliever that there might be something to the idea of visitation by space people. Despite Art Linkletter's own comment that aeronautical researcher William Lear (a personal friend of his) emphatically endorsed the existence of flying saucers, Mr. Robe insisted he had to have more proof to consider the matter seriously. Unknown to those on stage (except, of course, Art Linkletter), had Mr. Robe agreed there was some possibility, however slight, that UFO's were real, he would have won $1,000! Appropriately, as Art Linkletter warned the audience against such blind skepticism toward the saucer subject, a saucer glided Earthward in the background. Fitting indeed was Linkletter's closing quotation: "There are stranger things in heaven and Earth than are found in your philosophies."

SIGHTINGS OF INDEPENDENCE YOUTH

Mike Lyon, a young man of Independence, Mo., has seen some interesting UFO's the past three years.

His first sighting was when he and some friends were camping out. A pony had broken loose and he and his friends were catching him. They had the pony in a corner and the pasture became fairly bright with a light, and it was a dark night. The light hovered there for 15 or 20 minutes. He estimated it to be 400 to 500 feet high. They were leading the horse out through the pasture gate and when they turned to look again, the light was gone. The light was orange in color; he said it was bright enough to brighten up the pasture and you could make out things where you couldn't before because there was no moon or stars at all that night.

Later he had a second sighting which was pointed out to him by his younger sister. A light moved from north to south then paused for a moment, then it moved back north, then west to east and then moved back towards the house. It went at a very tremendous speed he said. As for the changes of direction, it just came to a stop and went in the other direction. This was not a bright object but more of a dull blue in the sky.

A third sighting occurred while Mike and his friends were driving down Lake City road. He said this light would follow while the radio was on but when they turned the radio off the light would quit. They turned on Truman Road, went over the hill and the light was resting over the Independence Power House. They decided to go towards Lake City and the light went towards Lake City. Then they followed it and it wasn't very fast. While this object was near, the radio had a lot of static on it, Mike said. This one was a reddish orange color.

A fourth one was while sleeping out in his back yard. He said it was very high and awfully slow. He was not sure of this one, said it could have been a plane. Since these sightings have been taking place, Mike occasionally is able to know what people are thinking before they say anything.

Recently he was in a Velvet Freeze ice cream place with friends and knew everything that would happen before it happened. He said it was like doing over again something he had already done.

READY TO FLEE LONDON
TV Science Fiction Panics Many Britons

London, Feb. 20. (AP)-Many Britons panicked tonight over a TV announcement that a space ship hovered with bombs over London.

"The prime minister has an announcement. . .London, the cabinet has decided, is to be evacuated. . ." (Continued)

It was the independent commercial network's dramatization of a play called "Before the Sun Goes Down" and viewers could see a motionless satellite hanging in the night sky. Or so they thought.

Women fainted.

TV switchboards were swamped with calls.

(This appeared in the Kansas City Times Saturday, Feb. 21, 1959)

Mitchell Sisters last speech, given January 11, in Drexel Hall, before UFO Study Club, is now available in mimeographed form---Price 50¢. Address your order to Paul M. Wheeler, 1117 W. Truman Road, Independence, Missouri.

NEW BOOKS FOR SALE: Reinhold Schmidt's new pocket edition of his experiences including his recent trip to the North Pole in a Flying Saucer---Price $1.35, plus the postage.

"Flying Saucers Are"---Bob Young's condensation of Buck Nelson's Convention, June 28, 29, 1958. Price 50¢, plus postage.

UFO LIBRARY: Two new books have been added to our Library and are available now. They are: "Transvaal Incident"---Anchor; "UFO Confidential"---Williamson & McCoy. It requires a deposit of $1.00 for members, or $2.50 for nonmembers. The club pays the postage one way and the borrower pays return postage. You may keep the books four weeks; after that a 4 cents per day fine is levied. Mail your deposit to Mr. A. Neal Pinkerton, Box 412, Kansas City 41, Mo. Or better yet, come to the next meeting and meet him and see the display.

vol. 1, No. 10   T H E   S P A C E V I E W E R   Dwight Bockman,
April, 1959   U.F.O. Study Club, Kansas City, Mo.   Editor

AUTHORITY TO GIVE TWO LECTURES

Dr. George Munt Williamson, anthropologist, lecturer, author, explorer and world traveler, will present TWO lectures on Sunday, April 12th, at 2:30 P.M. and 7:30 P.M. at Drexel Hall, Linwood and Baltimore, sponsored by the UFO Study Club of Kansas City. Dr. Williamson, who has just returned from a trip to South America, Europe and Great Britain, will present an afternoon lecture entitled THE LOST WORLD AND THE UFOs, and the evening lecture will be UFO WORLD REPORT. Both lectures are fully illustrated with colored slides.

Dr. Williamson served with the Army Air Corps during World War II as Radio Director for the Army Air Forces Technical Training Command. He received the Army Commendation Award from Brig. Gen. C. W. Lawrence for his outstanding record of service. He served as an instructor in anthropology for the United States Armed Forces Institute.

He attended Cornell College, Eastern New Mexico University, the University of Arizona, and took a special course at the University of Denver. He majored in anthropology in the northern part of the United States, Mexico, and Canada. He is an authority on Indian dances, music and ceremonial costuming. He is listed in "Who's Who In America" and "American Men of Science". He is presently head of the Department of Anthropology at Great Western University, San Francisco, California, and director of the Andean-Amazonian Field Station, Peru, South America.

Dr. Williamson is the author of a number of books including "The Hopi and Zuni Indians," "The Saucers Speak," "Other Tongues, Other Flesh," "Secret Places of the Lion," and "Road in the Sky."

Donation will be $1.00 for each lecture or $1.50 for both. Juniors 50 cents.

CHARLES BENNETT TO NEW POST

Charles Bennett, who has been making our tape recordings since the start of the Club, has been named Southwest Director of Tape Recorded UFO Information Service. This group is probably better known through its originator, Dr. A. G. Dittmar of Au Sables Fork, New York. As many members are already aware, Tape Recorded UFO Information Service is a non-profit organization distributing recorded material to UFO enthusiasts, sending in the necessary blank tape, postage, etc. Charles will be serving roughly the southeast quarter of the United States.

NOTICE--Change in tape copying policy: Charles Bennett regrets that increased recording expenses and lack of voluntary support make it necessary for him to charge a nominal fee for his copying service. Effective as of this publication, people requesting copies of the club lectures and other recordings (excluding TRUFO tapes) will be asked to contribute to the operation on the following basis--

     For those furnishing their own tape: 50 cents a reel for either 1,200' or
         1,800' tapes;
     For those desiring copies on low priced tape: $2.00 for 1,200' reels, $2.50
         for 1,800' reels, including service charge and purchasing expense.
     For those wanting copies on standard brands of recording tape: $2.50 for 1,200'
         reels, $3.75 for 1,800' reels (wholesale prices) plus the 50 cent copying
         fee.

If these more or less arbitrary rates work any hardships on people anxious to obtain recordings, exceptions can be made.

April, 1959   T H E   S P A C E V I E W E R   Page 2

LIEBETRAU LETTERS

February 24, 1959

Dear Bucky,

    Last evening I saw something which startled me so much that I was tempted to phone the KMBC news force and report this unusual spectacle. Because I'm only a housewife with little knowledge of these things, I was afraid my report would be of no importance and that I would merely be bothering them.

    This morning, however, I turned on my radio early hoping I would hear some logical explanation of what I had seen in the sky Monday evening at 7:00 o'clock. Imagine my surprise when the same, very large green and beautifully bright object had been seen by persons in Chicago, Wisconsin and Michigan, eleven hours later--at 6:30 a.m. Tuesday! They said it was the largest meteorite ever sighted. It was also talented, as it was traveling northwest when I saw it, and Chicago is northeast. And I'm just wondering why it took it eleven hours to travel such a short distance.

    I'm not implying it was a flying saucer for I didn't notice any portholes, smokestacks or peculiar exhausts.

    It just seems to me to have been "unmeteorite-like". And what happened to its tail? It moved through the sky like a giant green lantern--slowly and deliberately--not flashing across the heaven in a great hurry and leaving a trail of light behind it.

    Do you know anything about the proper behavior of meteorites that could help explain to me the antics of this particular one which cruised over our country for at least 11 hours last night?

                                                        Very sincerely,

    The above is a letter about a sighting on February 23, 1959, by Mrs. Liebetrau of 10821 W. 57th Terr., Shawnee, Kansas, to Bucky Walders, KMBC. The following letter was just received by Dwight and Lou Bockman:

March 23, 1959.

Dear Lou and Dwight,

    Last Wednesday evening, the 18th, was a warm night and I especially wanted to see a saucer. It was such a beautiful evening that I succumbed to the urge to let our supper go uncooked and take up my "sky watch" earlier than usual. I watch from the back porch step every evening for a while.

    Fred drove up around 7:30 or 8:00 and I told him that I was going to see a saucer and for him to come out and sit there with me.

    When he didn't come out I went inside and begged him, saying I knew I'd see one and wanted him to see it, too.

    He and Robin put on their coats and just as we stepped outside I looked up and said, "and there it is--see it!"

    Did you see the satellite go over K.C.? This looked just like the satellite--same size, same brightness--but it was traveling in the opposite direction although it was in the same location in the sky.

    We were looking southwest. The little, quiet, starlight object was traveling slowly in a nice straight path at an even speed.

    We kept moving around in the yard so that we wouldn't lose sight of it as it ducked behind our trees.

    It silently sailed towards the northwest until almost out of sight. I was about frantic to see more of it after I'd realized it wasn't a shooting star nor a plane. I began babbling out loud, "Oh, please, please come back--don't go away--" etc!

    It began to veer north and then northeast in a huge circle around our house ending up almost where we'd first noticed it and then it headed southwest and disappeared. I knew that was all.

                                                        Jane Liebetrau.

    Thanks, Jane.--And a word to all--Look up.

April, 1959　　　　T H E　S P A C E V I E W E R　　　　Page 3

LOCAL SIGHTINGS BY MR. ERIE

Dear Mr. Wheeler,

On Sunday, March 8, 1959, at approximately 8:20 p.m., my wife and I were driving north on S. 55th Street. We were at the Turner Fire Station at 55th and Metropolitan Avenue when I noticed a light off to the left and high in the sky, blinking red and white. It seemed to be stationary.

I kept watching it as I continued north to Kansas Avenue, and then I turned left across the bridge and river on my way to Muncie, Kansas. When I was in front of the Lake Park Drive-In Theater I stopped to see if the light was actually stationary or if my movement caused it to appear as such, but the light was stationary.

I continued on, keeping the light in sight until I got on 72nd Street going north, when I stopped on top of a hill to watch and then suddenly the light streaked across the sky for I judge a mile or mile and a half and then stopped and was again stationary. I continued on and after about two minutes I lost sight of it because of hills and such.

I continued on to 78th Street just south of the Kansas turnpike and never again sighted the light. I don't know what it was but I know it couldn't have been a plane because a plane couldn't move as fast as this light did, and then stop suddenly and hover. Also a plane couldn't have gone out of sight that fast, because the visibility was good.

　　　　　　　　　　　　　　　　　　　　　　　　　　Sincerely,
　　　　　　　　　　　　　　　　　　　　　　　　　　L. W. Erie

Thank you, Mr. Erie, of Muncie, Kansas.

HALSEY TEAM PROVIDED NEW FACET

A nice turnout enjoyed the lecture March 8 by Dr. Wallace C. Halsey. Others have given facts of contacts but Dr. Halsey gave us more of space philosophy--a vital message that gave us a better understanding of what we are supposed to do. Dr. Halsey was accompanied by his lovely wife, Terna, and Mr. Ray Barnes, editor of Searchlighter, the publication of Christ Brotherhood, Inc. Dr. Halsey is president of Christ Brotherhood, Inc. This trio departed for other missions, but left with us a warm friendship of brotherhood.

BOONVILLE SIGHTING

On the evening of April 17, 1958, an object was sighted over Boonville, Missouri. Among those who watched the object were Mrs. Riepe, post supervisor of the Sky Watch team, Ground Observer Corps, and several of her sky watchers.

Miss Peggy Leathers, who is one of the observers, called Mrs. Riepe about 6:50. Mrs. Riepe then watched it through binoculars for about twenty minutes, then called the report in to the St. Louis center.

When Mrs. Riepe first looked, the object appeared as a huge star, having a white fluorescent color. Using the binoculars she said it resembled a child's top. It was very high. At first it appeared to be completely still, but on aligning it with something on the ground she could see that it did have a slight drift with it.

It had a bright band about it, and some of the observers saw a dark spot in the bright band that seemed to rotate.

After several minutes of remaining almost still it suddenly turned fiery red and moved away at a fast rate of speed.

Others who watched included Peggy Leathers, Bill Davis, Bobby Frazier, Roger Land and Floyd Hansett, all teen-age observers.

MYSELF

　　In the Sacred Silence
　　　　Sometime quite unaware
　　We chance upon a stranger--
　　　　We find our real self there!
　　　　　　　　--Florence Maltby.

April, 1959 THE SPACEVIEWER Page 4

MEMBERSHIP DUES

Effective April 12, membership dues will be advanced to $2.00 for adults and $1 for juniors. Cards will be good through June, 1960. New members taking out membership at this time will gain the advantage of 2 months benefits.

SPECIAL MEETING

A special meeting will be held during intermission of the afternoon lecture, April 12, for the purpose of electing a nominating committee. This committee is for the purpose of selecting nominees for the executive board to be voted on at the annual meeting the second Sunday in June.

KEN PRIEST TO HEAD TAPE LIBRARY

The executive board has appointed Mr. Ken Priest as Tape Recording Librarian. Mr. Priest will set up the tape library to include club lectures, local sightings, TRUFO recordings, and others as available. Lending of these tapes will be carried out in a manner similar to the book library. Contributions will be accepted for this library as well as the book library. For further information contact Ken at CL4-5178, or write to 3001 Norton, Independence, Missouri

HARRIS SIGHTING

Mr. and Mrs. Dick Harris were returning to Kansas City from an outing one night last summer when they noticed a light following them. They had come through Norborne, Missouri, and were driving toward Hardin.

There is a straight stretch of road that runs about nine miles, and about the time they got on this straight stretch of road, Mr. Harris noticed a light following behind, possibly 150 to 250 yards back.

After a few miles of watching it through the rear view mirror he asked Mrs. Harris to look back to see what it was. She could not tell, and thought the back glass of their car might be distorting a light, so she put her head out of the window to see it. When she did this the object immediately moved back what they believed to be a mile or two.

They were, of course, amazed. While they were discussing it the object came back up close again.

Mrs. Harris had a cigarette in her hand and she struck a match to light it. As soon as she struck the match the object moved back a mile or so again. This puzzled them further.

By this time they were approaching the town of Hardin, and the first car they met on this road was coming toward them, and the object was raising out of their vision through the rear window.

They stopped the car, got out, and watched the object gain speed, and go at a terrific speed angling up, across the town of Hardin and out of sight.

Mr. and Mrs. Harris are both printers and have been with the Kansas City Times for many years.

Return to:
Paul M. Wheeler, President
U F O Study Club
1117 West Truman Road
Independence, Mo.

UFO STUDY CLUB
KANSAS CITY

vol. I, No. 10   T H E   S P A C E V I E W E R   Dwight Bockman,
April, 1959   U.F.O. Study Club, Kansas City, Mo.   Editor

==

AUTHORITY TO GIVE TWO LECTURES

Dr. George Munt Williamson, anthropologist, lecturer, author, explorer and world traveler, will present TWO lectures on Sunday, April 12th, at 2:30 P.M. and 7:30 P.M. at Drexel Hall, Linwood and Baltimore, sponsored by the UFO Study Club of Kansas City. Dr. Williamson, who has just returned from a trip to South America, Europe and Great Britain, will present an afternoon lecture entitled THE LOST WORLD AND THE UFOs, and the evening lecture will be UFO WORLD REPORT. Both lectures are fully illustrated with colored slides.

Dr. Williamson served with the Army Air Corps during World War II as Radio Director for the Army Air Forces Technical Training Command. He received the Army Commendation Award from Brig. Gen. C. W. Lawrence for his outstanding record of service. He served as an instructor in anthropology for the United States Armed Forces Institute.

He attended Cornell College, Eastern New Mexico University, the University of Arizona, and took a special course at the University of Denver. He majored in anthropology in the northern part of the United States, Mexico, and Canada. He is an authority on Indian dances, music and ceremonial costuming. He is listed in "Who's Who In America" and "American Men of Science". He is presently head of the Department of Anthropology at Great Western University, San Francisco, California, and director of the Andean-Amazonian Field Station, Peru, South America.

Dr. Williamson is the author of a number of books including "The Hopi and Zuni Indians," "The Saucers Speak," "Other Tongues, Other Flesh," "Secret Places of the Lion," and "Road in the Sky."

Donation will be $1.00 for each lecture or $1.50 for both. Juniors 50 cents.

CHARLES BENNETT TO NEW POST

Charles Bennett, who has been making our tape recordings since the start of the Club, has been named Southwest Director of Tape Recorded UFO Information Service. This group is probably better known through its originator, Dr. A. G. Dittmar of Au Sables Fork, New York. As many members are already aware, Tape Recorded UFO Information Service is a non-profit organization distributing recorded material to UFO enthusiasts, sending in the necessary blank tape, postage, etc. Charles will be serving roughly the southeast quarter of the United States.

NOTICE--Change in tape copying policy: Charles Bennett regrets that increased recording expenses and lack of voluntary support make it necessary for him to charge a nominal fee for his copying service. Effective as of this publication, people requesting copies of the club lectures and other recordings (excluding TRUFO tapes) will be asked to contribute to the operation on the following basis--

     For those furnishing their own tape: 50 cents a reel for either 1,200' or 1,800' tapes;

     For those desiring copies on low priced tape: $2.00 for 1,200' reels, $2.50 for 1,800' reels, including service charge and purchasing expense.

     For those wanting copies on standard brands of recording tape: $2.50 for 1,200' reels, $3.75 for 1,800' reels (wholesale prices) plus the 50 cent copying fee.

If these more or less arbitrary rates work any hardships on people anxious to obtain recordings, exceptions can be made.

April, 1959   T H E   S P A C E V I E W E R   Page 2

LIEBETRAU LETTERS

February 24, 1959

Dear Bucky,

Last evening I saw something which startled me so much that I was tempted to phone the KMBC news force and report this unusual spectacle. Because I'm only a housewife with little knowledge of these things, I was afraid my report would be of no importance and that I would merely be bothering them.

This morning, however, I turned on my radio early hoping I would hear some logical explanation of what I had seen in the sky Monday evening at 7:00 o'clock. Imagine my surprise when the same, very large green and beautifully bright object had been seen by persons in Chicago, Wisconsin and Michigan, eleven hours later--at 6:30 a.m. Tuesday! They said it was the largest meteorite ever sighted. It was also talented, as it was traveling northwest when I saw it, and Chicago is northeast. And I'm just wondering why it took it eleven hours to travel such a short distance.

I'm not implying it was a flying saucer for I didn't notice any portholes, smokestacks or peculiar exhausts.

It just seems to me to have been "unmeteorite-like". And what happened to its tail? It moved through the sky like a giant green lantern--slowly and deliberately--not flashing across the heaven in a great hurry and leaving a trail of light behind it.

Do you know anything about the proper behavior of meteorites that could help explain to me the antics of this particular one which cruised over our country for at least 11 hours last night?

Very sincerely,

The above is a letter about a sighting on February 23, 1959, by Mrs. Liebetrau of 10821 W. 57th Terr., Shawnee, Kansas, to Bucky Walders, KMBC. The following letter was just received by Dwight and Lou Bockman:

March 23, 1959.

Dear Lou and Dwight,

Last Wednesday evening, the 18th, was a warm night and I especially wanted to see a saucer. It was such a beautiful evening that I succumbed to the urge to let our supper go uncooked and take up my "sky watch" earlier than usual. I watch from the back porch step every evening for a while.

Fred drove up around 7:30 or 8:00 and I told him that I was going to see a saucer and for him to come out and sit there with me.

When he didn't come out I went inside and begged him, saying I knew I'd see one and wanted him to see it, too.

He and Robin put on their coats and just as we stepped outside I looked up and said, "and there it is--see it!"

Did you see the satellite go over K.C.? This looked just like the satellite--same size, same brightness--but it was traveling in the opposite direction although it was in the same location in the sky.

We were looking southwest. The little, quiet, starlight object was traveling slowly in a nice straight path at an even speed.

We kept moving around in the yard so that we wouldn't lose sight of it as it ducked behind our trees.

It silently sailed towards the northwest until almost out of sight. I was about frantic to see more of it after I'd realized it wasn't a shooting star nor a plane. I began babbling out loud, "Oh, please, please come back--don't go away--" etc!

It began to veer north and then northeast in a huge circle around our house ending up almost where we'd first noticed it and then it headed southwest and disappeared. I knew that was all.

Jane Liebetrau.

Thanks, Jane.--And a word to all--Look up.

April, 1959   T H E   S P A C E V I E W E R   Page 3

LOCAL SIGHTINGS BY MR. ERIE

Dear Mr. Wheeler,

On Sunday, March 8, 1959, at approximately 8:20 p.m., my wife and I were driving north on S. 55th Street. We were at the Turner Fire Station at 55th and Metropolitan Avenue when I noticed a light off to the left and high in the sky, blinking red and white. It seemed to be stationary.

I kept watching it as I continued north to Kansas Avenue, and then I turned left across the bridge and river on my way to Muncie, Kansas. When I was in front of the Lake Park Drive-In Theater I stopped to see if the light was actually stationary or if my movement caused it to appear as such, but the light was stationary.

I continued on, keeping the light in sight until I got on 72nd Street going north, when I stopped on top of a hill to watch and then suddenly the light streaked across the sky for I judge a mile or mile and a half and then stopped and was again stationary. I continued on and after about two minutes I lost sight of it because of hills and such.

I continued on to 78th Street just south of the Kansas turnpike and never again sighted the light. I don't know what it was but I know it couldn't have been a plane because a plane couldn't move as fast as this light did, and then stop suddenly and hover. Also a plane couldn't have gone out of sight that fast, because the visibility was good.

                                        Sincerely,
                                        L. W. Erie

Thank you, Mr. Erie, of Muncie, Kansas.

HALSEY TEAM PROVIDED NEW FACET

A nice turnout enjoyed the lecture March 8 by Dr. Wallace C. Halsey. Others have given facts of contacts but Dr. Halsey gave us more of space philosophy--a vital message that gave us a better understanding of what we are supposed to do. Dr. Halsey was accompanied by his lovely wife, Terna, and Mr. Ray Barnes, editor of Searchlighter, the publication of Christ Brotherhood, Inc. Dr. Halsey is president of Christ Brotherhood, Inc. This trio departed for other missions, but left with us a warm friendship of brotherhood.

BOONVILLE SIGHTING

On the evening of April 17, 1958, an object was sighted over Boonville, Missouri. Among those who watched the object were Mrs. Riepe, post supervisor of the Sky Watch team, Ground Observer Corps, and several of her sky watchers.

Miss Peggy Leathers, who is one of the observers, called Mrs. Riepe about 6:50. Mrs. Riepe then watched it through binoculars for about twenty minutes, then called the report in to the St. Louis center.

When Mrs. Riepe first looked, the object appeared as a huge star, having a white fluorescent color. Using the binoculars she said it resembled a child's top. It was very high. At first it appeared to be completely still, but on aligning it with something on the ground she could see that it did have a slight drift with it.

It had a bright band about it, and some of the observers saw a dark spot in the bright band that seemed to rotate.

After several minutes of remaining almost still it suddenly turned fiery red and moved away at a fast rate of speed.

Others who watched included Peggy Leathers, Bill Davis, Bobby Frazier, Roger Land and Floyd Hansett, all teen-age observers.

MYSELF

In the Sacred Silence
  Sometime quite unaware
We chance upon a stranger--
  We find our real self there!
        --Florence Maltby.

April, 1959   THE SPACEVIEWER   Page 4

MEMBERSHIP DUES

Effective April 12, membership dues will be advanced to $2.00 for adults and $1 for juniors. Cards will be good through June, 1960. New members taking out membership at this time will gain the advantage of 2 months benefits.

SPECIAL MEETING

A special meeting will be held during intermission of the afternoon lecture, April 12, for the purpose of electing a nominating committee. This committee is for the purpose of selecting nominees for the executive board to be voted on at the annual meeting the second Sunday in June.

KEN PRIEST TO HEAD TAPE LIBRARY

The executive board has appointed Mr. Ken Priest as Tape Recording Librarian. Mr. Priest will set up the tape library to include club lectures, local sightings, TRUFO recordings, and others as available. Lending of these tapes will be carried out in a manner similar to the book library. Contributions will be accepted for this library as well as the book library. For further information contact Ken at CL4-5178, or write to 3001 Norton, Independence, Missouri

HARRIS SIGHTING

Mr. and Mrs. Dick Harris were returning to Kansas City from an outing one night last summer when they noticed a light following them. They had come through Norborne, Missouri, and were driving toward Hardin.

There is a straight stretch of road that runs about nine miles, and about the time they got on this straight stretch of road, Mr. Harris noticed a light following behind, possibly 150 to 250 yards back.

After a few miles of watching it through the rear view mirror he asked Mrs. Harris to look back to see what it was. She could not tell, and thought the back glass of their car might be distorting a light, so she put her head out of the window to see it. When she did this the object immediately moved back what they believed to be a mile or two.

They were, of course, amazed. While they were discussing it the object came back up close again.

Mrs. Harris had a cigarette in her hand and she struck a match to light it. As soon as she struck the match the object moved back a mile or so again. This puzzled them further.

By this time they were approaching the town of Hardin, and the first car they met on this road was coming toward them, and the object was raising out of their vision through the rear window.

They stopped the car, got out, and watched the object gain speed, and go at a terrific speed angling up, across the town of Hardin and out of sight.

Mr. and Mrs. Harris are both printers and have been with the Kansas City Times for many years.

Return to:
Paul M. Wheeler, President
U F O Study Club
1117 West Truman Road
Independence, Mo.

Vol. 1, No. 11 THE SPACEVIEWER Dwight Bockman,
May, 1959   U.F.O. Study Club, Kansas City, Mo. Editor

DR. ROY PARSONS HERE MAY 6

Our May meeting will be held on Wednesday evening, May 6th, at 7:30 p.m. at Drexel Hall, Linwood and Baltimore, with Dr. Roy Parsons of Des Moines, Iowa, as our speaker. Dr. Parsons was born and raised in St. John's, Newfoundland, was ordained with the Methodist Church in Newfoundland. When he came to the United States he became a Baptist minister and pastored for some time the First Baptist Church of East New York. Later he became an independent minister and evangelist not affiliated with any denomination. He has been pastor of Fellowship Tabernacle-World Church in Des Moines for some five years. It is an independent, autonomous church, incorporated with the state of Iowa.

Dr. Parsons says that he has been having contacts with the space brothers since October, 1957, and is still having them. He claims to have several mementos of his contacts but cannot promise to bring them as he says he has to have "permission" first.

Mrs. Parsons, who will accompany Dr. Roy Parsons, was born and raised in Los Angeles, California. She attended the University of California for several years, majoring in music. Dr. Parsons says that while she has not been with him on his experiences in space ships and trips to other planets, she is able to tell many interesting and unusual incidents that have proved to her the validity of his experiences. Donation - $1.00 adults, 50¢ junior.

"ANOTHER CAYCE LECTURE"

On May 14th Lydia Schraeder Gray of the Association for Research and Enlightenment, Inc., of Virginia Beach, Virginia (Edgar Cayce Foundation) will speak in a public lecture at 8 P.M. at Drexel Hall, Linwood and Baltimore, on the subject, "Physical & Psychological Karma". Mrs. Gray is the author of "Children of the New Age". Admission will be $1.00.

THEOSOPHICAL SOCIETY MEET

On May 10th the Theosophical Society of Kansas City will present Miss Clara Codd, international lecturer and world traveler in a lecture entitled "How We Create Our Destinies," at 3 p.m. in the Warwick Room of the Pickwick Hotel. Miss Codd personally knew many of the early leaders of the Theosophical Society, and has spent many years in India, South Africa, and Australia. A native of England, Miss Codd was one of the first workers in woman suffrage in England.

DR. WILLIAMSON GAVE TWO LECTURES

On April 12, Dr. George Hunt Williamson gave two of the finest lectures this club has yet been blessed with. Like other speakers, Dr. Williamson willingly and uncomplainingly gave of his services and departed with little money to compensate for his great efforts. He made this lecture at a very busy time, just ahead of departing for Peru where he will continue his important research. With people like Dr. Williamson, his lovely wife and young son, going to great inconveniences to bring us their fine work, we owe them a debt of gratitude that we can pay only by increasing our own efforts. Let us, as true searchers, resolve to boost our efforts and attendance to the point where Drexel Hall won't hold us all.

U.F.O. REPORTS REQUESTED

Several nice reports on UFO's in the area have been documented. They have been advanced to you in past issues of the Spaceviewer. If you have seen a UFO please let us know about it. Write a letter telling about it to Dwight Bockman, 16207 E. 17th Street, Independence, Mo., or call CLifton 2-0814. We need your reports for documenting the local sightings. Also we would like to make tape recordings of interviews of your sightings.

SOUTH AMERICAN NEWSPAPER TRANSLATION

Society in Buenos Aires Affirms That Inhabitants From Venus, Jupiter and Mars Will Come to Earth This Year. By Alfredo Margenat.

"El Mundo"--(San Juan Puerto Rico News), March 5, 1959.--The "Association of Universal Metaphysics" that has its headquarters in Buenos Aires, Argentina, announces that during the course of this year 1959 inhabitants from Mars, Venus and Jupiter will launch on the Earth with the purpose of interviewing men of science, professors and newspaper men and explain their purposes of fraternity and peace with earth people.

This is what the president of said association, Mr. A. Millan, who lives at Alsina 1645 G, Buenos Aires, Argentina, South America, tells in a letter to EL MUNDO (Newspaper).

Regarding the desired trips to the Moon, the president of the universalists of Buenos Aires says the following:

"With due respect and admiration for the North American, German, Russian and English scientists we must tell you that such a launching will be impossible. The missiles will not be able to come in because as soon as they get close to a certain zone in the atmosphere or surrounding rings of those planets, they will be disintegrated without being able to send any warnings.

The leader of the association of Flying Saucers brings out the point that only very highly developed beings, or the inhabitants of those very planets can enter those planets."

He warns that only those who come with the purpose of fraternity, peace and love can enter the moon or other planets from the Earth.

Mr. Millan sends various newspaper clippings, among them some from EL MERIDIANO (the Meridian) edited in Cordoba, Argentina. In them are various reports that "soon we will again see the wonderful and flashing space ships through Cordoba, Buenos Aires, Mendosa, Salta, LaPampa, San Luis and San Antartico, and that several of these ships will be of a purple color.

In these space ships will come beings from other planets as peace ambassadors and they "will also come to bring scientific progress and spiritual progress attained in their worlds to cooperate with the earth's progress."

In El Meridiano newspaper it is announced that showers of meteors will fall on Earth to announce the great events of interplanetary nature that is drawing near.

The metaphysicians from this Group of Flying Saucers announce that the first ones in arriving here will be the inhabitants from Mars, Jupiter, and Venus. Among their purposes in coming here to Earth is the one of warning the earth people of the great danger that is involved in using atomic energy in atomic tests, hydrogen bombs, uranium and also those launchings to the moon.

The metaphysicians from Buenos Aires want to impress upon us the idea that those inhabitants from other planets will not come with aggressive ends to Earth but "with the only interest in fraternizing with the inhabitants of our planet."-- Contributed by Neal Pinkerton--translated for him by a friend (original clipping in Spanish). Thanks, Neal, and friend.

ORCHIDS TO HENSEVELT!

Our Librarian, Neal Pinkerton, reports that Ben Hensevelt, Lexington, Mo., heads the list of those who have contributed books for the library. To date, Mr. Hensevelt has donated sixteen books. All have had interesting titles and were in excellent condition, as new as though they had come direct from the publishers!

Our club library is steadily growing; and all members who happen to have books to share with other readers are reminded that each book is received with much appreciation, as the funds for the purchase of newsbooks are rather limited.

MYSTERIOUS LIGHT INTRIGUES HUNDREDS

For more than eight weeks viewers by the hundreds have gone to a place on Sac River some 10 miles east of El Dorado Springs, Mo., to watch a mysterious light that moves about the area almost every night.

The light has appeared in different places, and in different patterns of performance. Also it refuses to conform to any time pattern as it may appear early one night and late the next.

These are findings from interviews of a number of people in ElDorado Springs, April 1. Among those interviewed were Mr. C.A. Hendricks who operates an insurance agency there; Mr. Clarence Parsley, a printer, his wife and daughter, Beverly; Mr. Noble Carter, a grocer; Mr. Evans of Evans Drug; the high school principal, Mr.

Royce, and high school students, Charles Spicer, Sharon Boswell, Danny Gann, Raymond Flieschman, Jim Dislon, Laurel Mays and Richard Jackson.

Mr. Hendricks reported, "I was out there a week or ten days ago and there were probably 40 or 50 people watching for this light they had seen in the past, and about 10:15 the light did appear close to the river at Vilhower's Bluff. It appeared to be about 18 feet in the air. It was blinking at regular intervals. It was a bright red and it was on for approximately 10 to 15 seconds and it blinked about 6 or 7 times. It seemed to have traveled about half a quarter of a mile in that length of time. It appeared about 5 minutes later going in the opposite direction and it blinked about 3 times and went out. It blinked at regular intervals and was bright red. It looked something like a beacon light. It was below the timber line and appeared to be hanging there in mid air, blinking and traveling at a fast rate of speed."

Mr. Hendricks' daughter had previously seen the light. She told him it blinked once up a ways, blinked again down close to the ground, then blinked 4 or 5 times while traveling parallel and went out. She said it blinked at steady intervals.

The term "blinking" was described as equal intervals of which it was visible and of which it was not visible.

Mr. Clarence Parsley, a printer with the Witt Printing Co., reported seeing it on two different nights. He said, "At first it was a bright light and it wasn't moving. Then after a while it turned to a bright red, and went to flashing on and off like a patrol car, and moving to the east." He said it disappeared for a few seconds and then re-appeared about half a quarter of a mile east of the previous position. Then it made another appearance to the south with the appearance of being some 2 or 3 feet above the ground and in the road."

Five days later, according to Mr. Parsley's report, he returned to the area and viewed it again. He also said a large group of people saw it that night. He said, "That time it was just below the timber line. It was going east across the bottom field toward Blackjack. Four fellows took out running and tried to catch it, but they didn't have any luck."

A little later this same evening it appeared about one-eighth of a mile from the watchers and drifted to the southeast until it got to the edge of the timber. It stopped for a little bit, started dropping and was flashing as it dropped. It gave the appearance of hitting the ground and went out."

Reports indicate the light or object was round and appeared about the size of a volley ball. It has been reported as a green light. Has traveled different speeds, over a wide area and all the way from close to the ground to tree-top level. On one night the report gave 5 lights at one time. Some reports gave lights that were steady and did not blink.

The people of El Dorado Springs are very cordial and cooperative. If club members wish to go down there some night to sky-watch, addresses and phone numbers can be had by calling Dwight Bockman, CLifton 2-0814. It should be easy to arrange for someone in ElDorado Springs to accompany you or direct you to the area.

To the fine people of ElDorado Springs, our thanks.

McFARLAND SIGHTING NEAR JEFFERSON CITY, 1957

Question: Mr. McFarland, I understand you saw an interesting light in the sky some two years ago.

Mr. McFarland: "Well, it wasn't exactly a light, it was a flying object of some type. I was coming back on my vacation. It was around the second week of October, 1957. We were pretty close to Drake, just a little bit the other side of Drake, between Mt. Sterling and Drake on Highway 50 East. I noticed it in the sky and told my wife, and asked what she thought it was. She said nothing but a cloud, so I continued on. So I got where you turn off to a little town there, I forget the name of the town. I pulled up to a little gas station, got out and looked up at the sky. It was about 4 or 4:30 in the afternoon. We all got out. My wife took a look at it and so did my two children. They both recognized it as a cigar shaped object with a reddish flame streaking out the back of it. It was, I'd say 5,000 to 10,000 feet high, I don't know exactly. Of course I don't gauge distance too well. It was about half a mile from us. We watched it for about 5 minutes and it was going at an enormous rate of speed because I could gauge it by the ground it was covering. And all of a sudden it made a 90 degree turn and went straight up, and it disappeared. That's the last we ever saw of it. We went on into Jefferson City. We got there about 5:30 or 6, and reported it to the state patrol at the main office, to Highway Patrol Troop Headquarters, and they filed it, they said. That's all I ever heard of it. If you want to collaborate my statement you can get hold of my wife. I live at 402 North Ridgeway, Jefferson City, Mo., and my phone number is 65785."

He described the flame appearance leaving the object as being reddish orange, but the object itself being a silver color. Mr. McFarland operates a wholesale route out of Jefferson City for radio and television parts. (My apologies, Mr. McFarland, for failing to get your initials--Guess I became too interested in your sighting.) Thank you, Mr. McFarland for an interesting interview.

SLOW OBJECT OVER ELDORADO SPRINGS

On the evening of April 1, 1959, at 10 minutes til 7, three people watched an object go slowly over ElDorado Springs, Mo. They were Mr. Evans, owner of Evans Drug Store; Sharon Boswell, an employee, and Charles Spicer. They reported the object as being extremely high and moving in a southeasterly direction at a fairly slow speed. They believed it to be tremendous in size. It appeared as a bright star for about 5 minutes, then turned red for about 5 minutes, then back to white again for about 5 minutes. By this time it was diminishing and the three stopped watching it.

At the time this was taking place an interview was under way pertaining to the mystery light east of there. The interviewer returned to the Evans Drug Store immediately following this interview and was immediately informed of the sighting which had only a minute or two before ended.

* * * * * * * * * * * *

Vol. 1, No. 12　　　　　T H E S P A C E V I E W E R　　　　　Dwight Bockman,
June, 1959　　　　　　U.F.O. Study Club, Kansas City, Mo.　　　　　Editor

JUNE MEETING WILL BE HELD AT KANSAS CITY MUSEUM
SUNDAY, JUNE 14, 2:30 P. M.

Election of officers will take place at this meeting. All members are urged to be present. It is your responsibility to help guide the future of this club with your voice and vote. Of special interest will be a talk by DeLaverne Owen, one of our well-known members. Also our president, Mr. Paul Wheeler, will present a review of the past year's accomplishments of the club with a look into the future. No admittance charge will be made at this meeting. Memberships which are now due may be paid at this time. Remember, the place is Kansas City Museum, 3218 Gladstone Blvd. The date is June 14; the time is 2:30 P.M.

REPORT SEEING ESPECIALLY BRIGHT STAR
(Article taken from the Muskegon Chronicle, May 14, 1959)

Editor:

Somewhere I read that we "had some new stars in the heavens" but no one seems to know too much about them.

Early in May, about 9 p.m., I looked out to the western sky and saw one so big I almost tried to pick it. It was just like the Christmas stars that are pictured--six points with the bottom three about twice as long as the top three. I even called the neighbors out to look and watched the star for nearly an hour. Then had a kitchen errand for 10 minutes.

When I looked again, the star was making a hasty departure over Lake Michigan and to my knowledge has not returned.

It made me remember five years ago last winter when such a star was to be seen here and there for about two months. I found it outside my kitchen window one evening as I washed dishes. It seemed to have an intelligent control or to be manned by a personality. So, too, this one I saw recently.

My Bible says "In these days there will be strange things in the sky." How thrilled I am to be here now, when God is making his prophesies come alive before our very eyes.--Jessie M. Davis, 1878 Dowd St., Muskegon, Mich. Thanks to Mrs. Wm. L. Hubbard of Muskegon (the Wheeler's daughter), for turning this one in.

NEW CLUB FOR TOPEKA

On the afternoon of May 17 a group assembled at the home of Mrs. Deloris M. Trapp, 3315 Clare, Topeka, Kansas, and organized a saucer club. They decided on temporary officers with an election to be held soon. This method would also give them more time to select a name for the club, they reasoned.

Mrs. Trapp was made president and Mr. Harry Fleenor, 1033 Mulvane, secretary-treasurer. Other charter members are: Harold Wiseman, Dr. Albert Whiting, Mrs. Howard S. Searle, Melva Workman, Margaret Hersh, Harry Hardin and Mrs. Berneice Riley.

It is suggested that the clubs across the country add this club to your mailing list so that the Topeka UFO Club may have the enlightenment of your publications and releases.

We of Kansas City wish you pioneers a great success in enlightening your area. That the space brothers will shower you with an abundance of help is our prayer.

FLAMING BALL NEAR TOPEKA

The Topeka Daily Capital of May 2 carried a headline, "Flaming Ball Seen Falling Near Topeka." The Topeka Journal of May 2 carried a headline "Mystery Blaze Was Haystack."

The haystack report came from a Forbes Air Force dispatch which found the burning haystack at 1:00 a.m. The "flaming ball" was seen in the sky by at least five people; Mr. and Mrs. Walter L. Pennington, 1304 N. Central, Topeka; Mr. and Mrs. David Carreno, 3321 Pennsylvania, Topeka; and Miss Mary Passman, 318 South Cortland. They reported seeing the object at 10:10 p.m. This puts almost three hours between the sighting and the discovery of the burning haystack by the boys from Forbes.

Flaming Ball near Topeka (Continued)

Here is the story Mr. Walter Pennington gave us: "It was just a big ball of fire. It looked to me like it was 20 or 30 feet across. It was just a little bit longer coming down than it was across, but it was coming at an even speed. It didn't look like a meteorite because it wasn't going fast enough for one of those."..."It was coming down at about an 85 degree angle. We watched it a total of about 45 seconds before it disappeared behind the house."..."It seemed like it wouldn't be over 20 miles away at the most." ..."I'd say it wasn't moving over 200 miles an hour at the most from what I could see of it."..."It was 10 to 12 miles east of Hoyte, somewhere up there. That would be about 20 miles north of Topeka, somewhere in that neighborhood, and a little bit east of Highway 75."..."They found the haystack north of Holton six miles. So they were way off course between what we saw and where they found their fire."

Through another interview it was learned that Mr. and Mrs. David Carreno saw the same object, though they live on the opposite side of town from the Penningtons. They reported it as being high above ground, looked a little larger than the moon and was several miles away. Also that it was moving rather slow, and was red streaked, like flames. They, too, reported it as being in a northerly direction, and not in the vicinity of the haystack.

So now we got haystacks.

LOOKING BACK

After the busy month of April, having two lecturers, Mr. George H. Adamson on the 12th and Miss Dana Howard on the 26th, then on May 10th Dr. D. Roy Parsons, we feel we have had much food for thought and action. The experiences of these three people are all different, but the message they bring to us is one of light, truth and advancement to help us prepare ourselves for the new age that is being ushered in.

--L. W.

Remember, Ken Priest is in charge of our tape recording library. His phone number is CLifton 4-5178; address is 3001 Norton, Independence, Mo.

Vol. 2, Nos. 1 & 2   T H E   S P A C E V I E W E R   Dwight Bockman,
July & August, 1959   U.F.O. Study Club, Kansas City, Mo.   Editor
----

DR. WILLIAMSON TO RETURN

Dr. George Hunt Williamson is scheduled for a return engagement Sunday, August 2. Rather than the usual time this lecture will be held at 7:30 o'clock in the evening. Dr. Williamson has returned to the United States from Bolivia and Peru and has all new material. This lecture is entitled "City That Existed Before the Moon," and is fully illustrated with color slides.

Dr. Williamson is the anthropologist who lectured for us April 12. He gave us two very fine lectures that day and we expect this to be another outstanding lecture in the field of ufology.

Dr. Williamson served with the Army Air Corps during World War II as Radio Director for the Army Air Forces Technical Training Command. He received the Army Commendation Award from Brig. Gen. C. W. Lawrence for his outstanding record of service. He served as an instructor in anthropology for the United States Armed Forces Institute.

He attended Cornell College, Eastern New Mexico University, the University of Arizona, and took a special course at the University of Denver. He majored in anthropology in the northern part of the United States, Mexico, and Canada. He is an authority on Indian dances, music and ceremonial costuming. He is listed in "Who's Who In America" and "American Men of Science". He is presently head of the Department of Anthropology at Great Western University, San Francisco, and director of the Andean-Amazonian Field Station, Peru, South America.

Dr. Williamson is the author of a number of books, including "The Hopi and Zuni Indians," "The Saucers Speak," "Other Tongues, Other Flesh," "Secret Places of the Lion," and "Road in the Sky."

Donation will be $1.50 for this lecture. It will be held at Drexel Hall, Linwood and Baltimore. Remember, the time is 7:30 in the evening.

FINE WEATHER FOR PICNIC

The U.F.O. Club held a picnic Sunday, July 12, at Prairie Lee Lake. An area was reserved and the members gathered around 3 o'clock. It was a beautiful, mild day, neither too cool or too hot. It gave the 32 members attending a wonderful opportunity to become better acquainted and do some real visiting. Everyone brought food and a bountiful table was set and shared by all. Several remained until dark and viewed the craters on the moon through binoculars. Mrs. Frances Bennett made the arrangements and reservation, then our 1st vice president, Derrick Bennett, landed in the hospital with a virus infection. We missed you, Frances, Derrick, Charles and Emilie.

OVAL SHAPED OBJECT

A beautiful big bright pinkish-white object, appearing about eight times the size of Venus, was seen at 7:50 P.M. June 10, by Irene Schaeffer of 300 S. Bellaire, Kansas City, Mo. Mrs. Schaeffer spotted the oval shaped object and immediately called it to the attention of a neighbor, Mrs. E. L. Gahm, and her teenage daughter, Judy Gahm. The object had a luminescent quality, she said. It went toward the ground fast, like a meteor, then leveled off. Then it took a slight angle upward and traveled at a slower speed until it disappeared. Mrs. Schaeffer said she thought she watched it for at least 30 seconds.--Thank you, Irene.

IT COMES FROM THE HEART

Seems that higher authority has a way of bringing light in when the hour is the darkest. The hour of darkness was for Bob Young in leaving Buck Nelson's convention on Monday morning, June 30. The rays of light were Mr. and Mrs. Ben Hensevelt who departed the convention grounds after Bob did.

Bob is the printer writer, from Waterloo, Iowa, who covered Buck's convention last year and gave a report of it in a book called "The Saucers Are." He rode a motorcycle loaded to the very limit, including tape recorder, tent, clothes, food, printed matter, in fact, so much that it looked like a physical impossibility had been accomplished.   (Continued over)

This year was a repeat performance for Bob, but this time he had even more load. He carried two tape recorders.

All went well for Bob through the convention. He made his recordings, talked to the contactees, made special tape interviews and gained all the material he needed for his report again this year in book form.

But Monday was another story. He had started his trip to Waterloo, was on the highway some four miles east of Willow Springs, Mo., when the rear tire blew out. He was scooted or dragged about 75 feet. His back was scratched extensively, he received a hole in his side, a deep wound in his head and a hand was mangled to the extent that the leaders were showing.

Yes, this was a dark hour for a rugged individual. But it was not to remain dark for higher authority had played a role. Through hunches, intuition, or whatever you term that guiding force, Mr. and Mrs. Ben Hensevelt had felt a strong impelling force that urged them to delay their departure, and they did. This placed them several minutes behind Bob, so that shortly after it happened they came upon the accident.

The Hensevelts immediately took over, and after a word of prayer, emptied the load from the motorcycle into their pickup truck and took Bob to a clinic in Willow Springs.

Another fortunate incident was that a surgeon from Chicago happened to be visiting there at the time. This surgeon spent two hours patching up Bob's wounds.

At this point Mr. Hensevelt took a couple of men, returned to the scene of the accident and loaded the motorcycle into the pickup.

On returning to the clinic, Bob and the Hensevelts conferred, and decided to make the trip to Waterloo against the advice of the physicians who had advised six weeks in the hospital.

Mr. and Mrs. Hensevelt brought Bob to their home in Lexington for the night, then made the trip on to Waterloo the next day.

Needless to say the relationship established between the Hensevelts and all of Bob's relatives was wonderful. Needless to say such an action as this found the gold in someone else's heart.

We know you have been paid, Mr. and Mrs. Hensevelt. Paid in a portion of something money cannot comprehend. We know you will receive more such payment.

To you, Bob Young, man of fortitude, man with a cause, get well, real soon.

CONVENTION HIGHLIGHTS

Several persons of this area attended Buck Nelson's Spacecraft Convention at Mountain View, Mo., June 27 and 28.

A number of those present camped out at the convention site and enjoyed the camp fire atmosphere as they listened to speakers on Friday and Saturday nights, June 26 and 27.

Tape recordings of the convention were made by several people and will be available in the club's tape library.

One of the highlights of the convention was George King, chairman and founder of the Aetherius Society of England. He spoke relative to his communication with masters of other planets and urged universal peace through abandoning our atomic and hydrogen bomb tests. He also told how space people are helping us, such as: maintaining satellites to provide energies, charging mountains as New Age power centers, alleviating radioactivity, easing conditions, continuing the teachings of Jesus, and preparing the way for a forthcoming avatar.

Another high interest spot was Jim Velasquez (Ethe), of Santa Ana, California. He spoke of his psychic experiences with the "Lords of Light of Etheria," passing on information conveyed to him via a question process used by space people during subsequent telepathic contact. With a word directed especially to the contactees he made a plea to them to "clean up their ranks." He also explained music he has been given corresponding to the vibratory rates of colors, which he has on disc recordings, and told of forth coming volumes of New Age Proverbs which he has received and is putting into print. He has also had personal contacts.

(Continued next page)

The Mitchell sisters, of St. Louis, surprised us by saying they expect to move to Kansas City in the very near future. (A hearty welcome to you, Betty and Helen.) They both gave a talk and brought a message from the space contact from Venus recounting the history and prehistory of Earth showing lagging spiritual progress.

The speeches by the two Mitchell sisters are being mimeographed and will soon be available from Paul Wheeler, 1117 West Truman Rd., Independence, Mo. Price 50¢.

Space does not permit a complete coverage of the convention in this publication but here are the remaining speakers:

Fanny Lowery, Sherman Lowery, Bessie Arthur, Chief Standing Horse, Truman Bethrum, Prince Neosom, Russell Dilts, Nathan Baldwin, Paul Wheeler, Dana Howard, Wayne S. Aho, E. H. Blomberg, Alice Findling and James L. Hill.

BOOKS AVAILABLE FROM CLUB

The book, "The Saucers Are," by Bob Young, of Waterloo, Iowa, is still available through the club at 50 cents per copy. This book is a report of Buck Nelson's 1958 Convention. It can be obtained through Luella Wheeler, 1117 W. Truman Rd., Independence, Mo. Bob's new book, which will be a report on the 1959 Buck Nelson Convention, can be purchased in advance by sending 50¢ to Bob Young, Box 657, Waterloo, Iowa.

There are still some available copies of the speeches by the Mitchell sisters, given here last January 11.

ANOTHER CLUB PICNIC

Another club picnic is scheduled for Sunday, August 9, at Budd Park, located at Hardesty and St. John Avenue. An area has been reserved for 2:30 O'clock. There is a wading pool for children under 14. This is another pot luck affair where we spread the food all together. This is for all members and their friends and presents an excellent way of getting better acquainted. We plan to eat at 5:30.

LOS ANGELES CONVENTION

About 2,000 people attended the convention of the Amalgamated Flying Saucer Clubs of America, held at the Statler-Hilton Hotel in Los Angeles, California, July 11 and 12. Host of the convention was Gabriel Green, director of the Amalgamation, and president of the Los Angeles interplanetary Study Group.

The entire second floor of this hotel was reserved for the occasion. Careful planning and much work by Mr. Green and his associates brought about a new approach in spacecraft conventions. About 50 speakers participated and six lecture halls were used simultaneously. This allowed the spectators to choose the speaker they wished to listen to at the particular time.

LATE FLASH

This one comes from Frances Bennett, just in time for publication. She received a letter from Bob Young of Waterloo, Iowa, telling of this sighting. Wednesday, July 15, approximately midnight, at Ingawanis Boy Scout Camp near Waverly, Iowa, a UFO was sighted for approximately 1 minute and described by the two boys and one Scout master. The object was noticed in west southwest at approximately 20 to 30 degrees in relation to earth. It was slightly oval, bright on the bottom and hazy on top, appeared to be the size of the moon and weaved slightly from side to side as it diminished its size down to nothing within a period of approximately one minute. Each one was interviewed by Bob Young the following morning.

QUOTING BILL VAUGHN - Star Beams, K.C. Star - 7-18-'59

The Air Force reports only half as many flying saucer sightings this year as last. Republicans say this is because times are so good everybody has his nose to the grind stone; Democrats say it's because times are so bad everybody has their eyes on the ground looking for dimes.

Comment: Could it also be that people are not reporting their sightings for fear of being labeled a crackpot, perhaps told that what they saw was a mirage or hallucination? -- L.W.

SUPPORT YOUR CLUB

Attendance at all club activities is a very essential part of it. Clubs just do not survive by remote control. For a club to grow and thrive it requires the participation of its members. This is an active and highly informative club and it is our individual responsibilities to keep it that way. We are on the inside, in the know on many things the public should know. Being in this position, we have a responsibility to the public under universal law. These responsibilities do not necessarily come easy or cheap. Let us resolve to make a showing in our attendance, urging all of our friends to attend, and get a new period of growth started that can go a long way toward enlightening Kansas City.

Dr. G. H. Williamson, who is one of our top authorities, will be with us at 7:30 in the evening, August 2. By all means remember this lecture. It will be an important highlight in the history of this club.

Vol. 2, Nos. 3 & 4   THE SPACEVIEWER   JULIA T. BROWN
Sept. & Oct., 1959   U.F.O. Study Club, Kansas City, Mo.   EDITOR

REVEREND MILTON NOTHDURFT

Reverend Milton Nothdurft is scheduled for our next lecture, Friday Evening, October 16th, at 7:30 o'clock. Reverend Nothdurft, of Maquoketa, Iowa, is an ordained Methodist minister, the son of a minister. He has had wide experience in religious work, especially with Youth groups. This lecture is entitled "Why the Confusion In Saucer Research"

Reverend Nothdurft holds a Bachelor of Arts degree from Cornell College (Iowa), Bachelor of Sacred Theology, Boston University School of Theology (seminary training for the ministry). Also Master of Sacred Theology, Boston University, School of Theology.

His interest in Saucers began even before the Kenneth Arnold episode. He read and subscribed to all the Science Fiction and Space magazines he could find. He numbers among his friends the most known of the contactees and researchers, although he isn't an actual contactee himself. While on a trip to the Holy Land in 1954 he met and had tea with Desmond Leslie in his apartment in London.

Reverend Nothdurft suggests that we take personal feelings out of our study of Flying Saucers and says, "Let us unite under the banner of the Prince of Peace."

This lecture will be held at Drexel Hall, Linwood and Baltimore, Kansas City. Remember the time is 7:30 in the evening. A donation of $1.50 will be taken.

International Convention at Des Moines, Iowa

An INTERNATIONAL Convention of the Universal Fellowship Order will be held at Des Moines, Iowa, on Friday, Saturday and Sunday, October 30, 31 and November 1, at the Fellowship Tabernacle, located in the 2600 block, S.E. 14th Street & Creston. For Reservations please write to Dr. Roy Parsons, Pastor of Fellowship Tabernacle, or Dr. Wallace C. Halsey, Associate Pastor, P.O. Box 150, Des Moines, Iowa. Be sure to state the number of your party who will attend.

A banquet is being planned for this occasion. Don't miss this most wonderful opportunity to get acquainted with the Parsons and Halseys and the work which is being started there. Make plans and reservations RIGHT NOW!

Directions for finding Fellowship Tabernacle: Leaving Kansas City, take Highway 69 north to Osceola, Iowa, then just north of Osceola about 1 mile, turn west 1 mile, to the Iowa State Freeway, then north to the Airport turn off at Des Moines, turn east and go 9 miles, to Highways 69 & 65, then north about 2 miles, to the 2600 block. A sign on west side of street, "Fellowship Tabernacle" points the way into the grounds.

UFO NACHRICHTEN   WIESBADEN, GERMANY

A UFO SAULUS TURNS INTO A PAULUS

Dr. Donald Menzel, Professor at Harvard University, U.S.A., for years a strong opponent to the opinion that UFO's are from other planets, left his Light Reflex and Hallucinations Theory, to join the front ranks for a positive UFO investigation. The reason: He recently had a sighting, which was for him absolutely convincing. Study groups, observing the same sighting, stated: One of the most clearly convincing sightings of the year.

We have been informed recently that the Mitchell Sisters plan a 4-page bulletin containing information from the Space Brothers. There will be a question and answer page. For particulars write to Helen and Betty Mitchell, 132 South Clark St., Ferguson 35, Mo.

For copies of the Mitchell Sisters' lectures of last January and the convention at Buck Nelson's, write to Mrs. Luella R. Wheeler, 1117 W. Truman Road, Independence, Missouri. They are 50¢ each.

For information concerning Tape Recordings of UFO Club speeches call or write Mr. Ken Priest, 3001 Norton, Independence, Mo. His telephone number is CL 4-4178.

Page Two

We wish to express our regrets over the recent resignation of Mr. Dwight Bockman as Editor of the Spaceviewer. We take this opportunity to express our appreciation for the wonderful job of editing you have done for us, Dwight.

Mrs. Julia Brogan, 3623 Windsor, Kansas City 23, Mo., has taken over the job. She has had quite a bit of training as a writer but to date has done more poetry than factual writing. She feels this will be a wonderful opportunity to learn. Welcome to our staff, Julia.

- - - - - - - - - -

A letter from Thelma Olson calling our attention to Miss Laura Taylo's recent visit to our meeting has been received. She lives for the summer at Moline, Kansas, which is 250 miles away. She came in Sunday morning and left on the midnight train after the lecture. She is very interested in Ufology. Miss Olson also calls our attention to the group which comes from Wichita. We understand the group is brought by Dr. Schmidt. Thank you, Miss Olson, for telling us.

- - - - - - - - - -

From Gladys Fusaro, Director of Intercontinental Aerial Research Foundation, New York, Luella Wheeler had a letter recently. Among other interesting things she said is, "I think if MORE concentration on our work in our particular fields was given instead of 'assassination' of personalities, their work and character, there would be more accomplished. It seems a shame the amount of jealousy and distrust that exists among certain ones in some of the groups. After all, we are ALL trying to work TOGETHER for a common cause, to find out the truth of the Enigma of the UFO's, and to find a way of better understanding of the way of Life, and this dissention certainly doesn't help the cause at all."

- - - - - - - - - -

From S U F O I, Denmark, Europe, May 20, 1959, comes:

"FLYING SAUCER MAN VISITS QUEEN JULIANA"

"Haag-RB--Reuter--Queen Juliana and Prince Bernhard received Monday the 68-year-old self-appointed California expert of flying saucers in a private audience at Castle Soestdijk, near Utrecht. The visit has been criticised by the Holland Press.

"Adamski, who is in Holland to report on his alleged meeting with inhabitants of Mars, has written a book titled THE FLYING SAUCERS HAVE LANDED. The American claims also that he has met inhabitants from Venus and has traveled to the moon. The audience lasted about an hour.

"The attache to the Queen said later that the meeting was arranged so the Royal couple could meet Adamski and learn more about his point of view. Commenting on the criticism of the meeting in several of the papers the attache reminded them that it is only the Queen's private affair who she receives in an audience.

"Amsterdam's leading Catholic newspaper said it 'has nothing against Adamski's audience if he was not considered as an astronomical philosopher, who has received wisdom from the inhabitants of Mars and Venus, whom nobody else has ever seen.'"

- - - - - - - - - -

N.Y.Times, July 29, 1959:

NEW RADAR SPOTS MAN CRAWLING TWO MILES AWAY

The army has developed a super-sensitive radar that can see and hear a soldier crawling on the ground 2 miles away, or spot a tank or jeep at ten miles. It says the gadget is so refined it can tell the difference between a man and a woman at more than 600 yards at night or in a fog.

An announcement today said the two-mile range for spotting a crawling soldier was under average conditions. Under ideal conditions in a test made in the desert, the surveillance radar spotted a soldier walking at fifteen miles. Army technicians noted that men were usually taller than women and showed pronounced differences in walk.

- - - - - - - - - -

PONTIAC, MICHIGAN, PRESS, August 18, 1959:

Two yellow discs hovered over the horizon and streaked across the sky, leaving a flaming trail of red and pink vapor. Reports of the sighting came from all over the Pontiac area. Witnesses say they first appeared about 7:30 P.M. and continued their 'eerie performance with a purpose' for about 20 minutes. Wanda Bierl, 405 Linda Vista Drive, tells about it:

"We were sitting in the car at a drive-in waiting for the show to begin while our three children were at the playground up front. It wasn't quite dark yet and suddenly my husband told me to look at those things in the lower horizon. We saw couples in other cars watching too, and some got out to look.

"There were two yellow discs in the sky, not in the heavens, but in our atmosphere. The two objects faced each other and for about 8 minutes stood perfectly still, except that when you looked at them very closely they looked like they were drifting with the wind and moving slightly. They moved separately and of their own accord. There wasn't a cloud in the sky and I couldn't find the moon.

"The next 3 minutes one moved higher and they stood there drifting in place. All of a sudden the lower one took off in a straight upward movement and became a very thin disc with a long, yellow tail, with a bit of red in it looking like a fire streak. Then, 30 seconds later, the second one moved up and over and down in a perfect arc, leaving a yellow trail behind it. It disappeared completely while the first disc continued to go straight up, then leveled off and began flying perfectly straight about 3 minutes, trailing to the right with a stream of yellowish reddish vapor that faded to pink as it disappeared. As the first one faded the second came back into view, looking like it was coming straight at us, right under the other which reappeared. They both arched together, making a big U-turn and streaked away. The objects had very distinct lines, except when they moved in a blurred flight. They were very distinct in movements, not like something fallen to earth. There was a human intelligence about the whole thing, or superhuman."

Local observatories and police could give no explanation for last night's occurrence. --(Thanks to Ruth & Al Korinek of Detroit.

- - - - - - - - - - - - - - - - -

This summer your new editor was fortunate enough to have a month's vacation in the West, with the focal point the Amalgamated Flying Saucer Clubs of America, Inc., convention at the Statler-Hilton Hotel, in Los Angeles. I asked Gabriel Green personally Sunday morning how many people were there and he said the count was about 2500 for Saturday but they didn't have a total yet for Sunday. It was a very wonderful experience. But if I had any criticism at all it would be they had too many things scheduled and we had to skip about too much. All of the ballroom floor was divided into meeting rooms, and I heard some marvelous speakers. But one can't be in six places at once, so I imagine I missed some I should have heard.

Going through the desert towards San Diego from Phoenix, when we got back in the bus from a rest stop about 2 A.M. the woman next to me called my attention to an extremely bright star. By then several of the others were watching it. It kept getting bigger and bigger until it was about the size of a silver dollar. Then it seemed to flip over on its side and just faded away. We were too astonished to speak for a minute as it all happened so suddenly. The same thing happened as I was crossing Utah toward Salt Lake City. I am convinced it was a saucer but it didn't come close enough for identification.

On Saturday afternoon of the meeting someone handed a newspaper to the speaker. In 2-inch letters, visible all over the room, he held up the Los Angeles Mirror News: MYSTERY SKY OBJECT SIGHTED OVER PACIFIC. When we could rush and get papers we found a "veteran pilot for Pan American World Airways reported he and his co-pilot saw an object with a mysterious cluster of extremely bright lights flashing past his plane over the Pacific, 'faster than anything I've ever seen.' Wilson said the object seemed to be bearing down on his plane but turned abruptly and lights disappeared. He said 'it made a believer of me.'"

I clipped items from several other Los Angeles papers, all about sightings during the convention. (Continued)

Page Four

In addition to the convention, I stopped a while at San Diego to dream by the ocean I had never seen; spent a day at Disneyland; ate fish down at Fisherman's Wharf in San Francisco after riding the cable-car down. I stopped off two weeks at Flagstaff, Arizona, to a writers' workshop and was fortunate to visit Mt. Lowell Observatory. That is the one that discovered Pluto. We saw Jupiter and three of his twelve moons. I heard the wonderful organ in a concert at the Mormon Temple in Salt Lake City. Truly a memorable vacation.

SUPPORT YOUR CLUB

Attendance at all club activities is a very essential part of it. Clubs just do not survive by remote control. For a club to grow and thrive it requires the participation of its members. This is an active and highly informative club and it is our individual responsibilities to keep it that way. We are on the inside, in the know on many of the things the public should know. Being in this position, we have a responsibility to the public under universal law. These responsibilities do not necessarily come easy or cheap. Let us resolve to make a showing in our attendance, urging all of our friends to attend, and get a new period of growth started that can go a long way toward enlightening Kansas City.

If you enjoy the SPACE VIEWER we hope you will keep your membership dues up to date. They are $2.00 a year. All donations are acceptable.

Remember the date of the next meeting, October 16, Friday evening at 7:30 at Drexel Hall. Speaker, the Reverend Milton Nothdurft of Maquoketa, Iowa, his subject, "Why the Confusion In Saucer Research". This will be the only notice sent out about this lecture, so mark it on your calendar NOW!!

Vol. 2, No. 8   T H E S P A C E V I E W E R   JULIA BROGAN
February 1960   UFO Study Club, Kansas City, Mo.   EDITOR
****

DR. D. ROY PARSONS OF DES MOINES, IOWA

The Unidentified Flying Objects Study Club of Kansas City is privileged to announce that Dr. D. Roy Parsons, minister and pastor of Fellowship Tabernacle of Des Moines, Iowa, will speak on the subject of Flying Saucers, their meaning and why they are here.

The meeting will be Sunday, February 14, at 2:30 p.m., at Drexel Hall, Linwood and Baltimore, in Kansas City, Missouri.

Dr. Parsons was born and raised in St. Johns, Newfoundland, where he was ordained a Methodist minister. When he moved to the United States he became a Baptist minister and served the First Baptist Church in east New York for a period of time.

Later he became an independent minister and evangelist, not affiliated with any church.

Dr. Parsons is now pastor of Fellowship Tabernacle---World Church, incorporated with the state of Iowa, where he has served the past five years. The name of this organization has now been changed to Universal Fellowship Order.

Dr. Parsons says that in his contacts with the "Space Brothers" he has been informed of many things of a universal nature which pertain to a way of life far beyond our own. He has been given information on the following subjects: 1. Cultural, 2. Political, 3. Religious, 4. Scientific, 5. Philosophical, 6. Psychological, and 7. Financial.

Dr. Parsons claims to have had contacts with the Space People since October, 1957, and is still having them.

Come and hear a fine lecture by a very dynamic speaker. The club is asking a donation of $1.50 for adults and 50¢ for juniors.

- -

Under Cosmic Law "All peoples are in their right places at the right time."--From UNDERSTANDING, October 1959.

- -

DISCOVER YOUR TRUE WORTH---by Albert Schweitzer

It's not enough merely to exist. It's not enough to say, "I'm earning enough to live and to support my family. I do my work well. I'm a good father. I'm a good husband. I'm a good churchgoer."
That's all very well. BUT YOU MUST DO SOMETHING MORE. Seek always to do some good, somewhere. Every man has to seek in his own way to make his own self more noble and to realize his own true worth.
You must give some time to your fellow man. Even if it's a little thing, do something for those who have need of a man's help, something for which you get no pay but the privilege of doing it. For remember, you don't live in a world all your own. YOUR BROTHERS ARE HERE TOO.--From "This Week Magazine" Nov. 29, 1959.

- -

We wish to acknowledge belatedly a letter from Mrs. Helen M. Boyd, 722 S.5th St. Rich Hill, Mo., reporting a sighting last July. Mrs. Boyd says:
"I just want to tell you I've at last been favored with a UFO sighting during daylight hours. It was about noon, July 1. I'd been down to the farm for some vegetables and was returning home when the reflection of the sun on this object caught my attention. About the turn of a car wheel distant, then the brilliance of the light was gone, leaving an extremely clear--not transparent--silver colored object not very high in the sky. Almost immediately it turned so I could better see its shape, which was disc, or saucerlike. I was approaching a bridge, yet I watched it 5 or 10 seconds, until I had crossed the bridge. When I stopped the car for a better study, nothing remained in the azure sky but a tiny puff of white cloud not even re-

(Cont. next page)

remotely near where I had seen the object. There was no sound. I was going north and this object was northeast of me. It really gave me a breathtaking experience!"

Thank you very much, Mrs. Boyd.

- -

We hope you noticed the article by Dr. Wernher von Braun on Immortality in the Sunday, January 24, THIS WEEK. In it he says--

"Science has found that nothing can disappear without a trace. Nature does not know extinction. All it knows is transformation.

"Now if God applies this fundamental principle to the most minute and insignificant parts of His universe, doesn't it make sense to assume that He applies it also to the masterpiece of His creation--the human soul? I think it does. And everything Science has taught me, and continues to teach me, strengthens my belief in the continuity of our spiritual existence after death. Nothing disappears without a trace."

Isn't that wonderful, coming from a 'factual' scientist?

- -

From the WEEKLY READER (used in the public schools) Jan. 18-22, news report we gleaned this:

"Scientists have had two five-minute 'conversations' with the planet Venus. The messages were hard to hear and even harder to understand. No wonder! Venus is about 28 million miles away!

"Scientists worked long and hard before they could be sure they had really 'talked' with another planet. It was the first time this had been done."

- -

This was sent us by Larry Lindvig from Chicago:

Excerpts from the Radio-TV columns in the DAILY NEWS report that Long John, WOR radio in New York, was in a heated discussion with James Mosely, Gray Barker and Ben Isquith about saucers when they were cut off the air and music played for the last hour of the program. That was August 29, 1959, "Around the Dials".

From "What's On?" December 31, 1959:

On another program Comedian Jackie Gleason was discussing saucers with Long John. Gleason thinks they come from other planets; he believes in extra-sensory perception; he is sold on ghosts and teleportation; and he's a true believer in religion. Gleason gave the listeners a truly fascinating glimpse of the character and mental makeup of one of the most unusual personalities before the public today."

Thank you Larry Lindvig.

- -

Excerpt from a column in "Midnight", NIGHT AND DAY IN MONTREAL CANADA, November 9, 1959, by Terry Taylor:

"Two American A.T. Intelligence men were in town last week from Washington, to see what they could do to hush up Flying Saucer revelations from the lips of Ronald Anstee."

This excerpt was sent to us by C. Alexander Odell, FILS., VSM. of "The World Institute of Inter-Galactic Cosmic Science" Canadian Chapter. Office address: P.O.B. 82, Port Elgin, N.B., Canada.

He says: "It has come to our attention that one of our worthy members, who is Director of Public Relations & Information, has been singled out as an object--apparently--by members of the Intelligence Department of the U.S. Air Force. It is respectfully pointed out that the U.S.A.F. has no jurisdiction over citizens of Canada, which is a member of the British Commonwealth of Nations and which contrary to some beliefs, is an independent sovereign state within that "family" of nations.

Moreover, there is NO censorship of news in Canada respecting the so-called UFO reports, nor over information respecting same. There is still a modicum of freedom in the Canadian press! Whether peoples in foreign governments like it or not, Canadians resent the interference by American, or, Britons, for example. Lip service to a particular cause or political doctrine is not a habit of Canadians, but, silent convictions appertaining to such causes or political leanings borne out in daily lives is the usual evidence of such convictions.

Recently two of your USAF Intelligence Officers have been reported by a local Montreal newspaper (see article by Terry Taylor) as having been in that city with a view to interfering with the right of free speech under British Justice in Canada. It is high time that our "friends" in your nation's government mind their own business and cease to interfere in the internal affairs of any particular nation--particularly that one nation on earth where Americans are more graciously received than in any other! We are drawing your attention to this one of several reports--which we take, prima facia, as being accurately reported from the context of the report. We are directing this letter and enclosure to you as one of the most serious and sincere groups in the U.S.A., through our able secretary (Mrs. Ethel Ash) who is also a member of your club, in the hope that you will adequately "air" this complaint over the network which we understand you are able to use for discussions on just such topics as these. The writer adds that owing to the numerous incidences similar, or, analagous to that herein mentioned, we have receded from considering forming a group in your country. There appears to be sufficient "groups" in the U.S.A., and we do not wish to add to the confusion existing there already."

A most unusual article from the SPACECRAFTER, Phoenix, Arizona, of October, 1959, has come to our attention. It is called FEAR and was written by Betty Eilers. She says:

"When future ages view our present age, can there be little doubt they will say, 'Why these people paid homage to a huge and monstrous god named FEAR!'.

"It is said that each generation is wiser than the one preceding it. Should we doubt that not only future beings on this planet, but that visitors from other planets, will read the horrible truth about our CULT of FEAR?

"Many of us were brought up by well-meaning parents to FEAR the Deity--in the same breath we were taught to LOVE our neighbors and parents. The third requirement was to LOVE God. How can love and fear co-exist?

"Do you ever think of the place of animals in this great Plan? Sirius, the Dog Star, watches over all from his serene home in Space.

"Some of us FEAR death. Can we be so enamoured of the paltry offerings of earth that nothing better awaits us?

"We fear old age; loss of employment; going to Hell at the time of death--but no one has shown the location of such a place! We fear 'what people will say'. There are sins of omission as well as commission.

"For fear of disease man will stoop to any method to relieve his pains--which he made mostly for himself.

"FEAR has driven nations to war; it is now costing billions of dollars in lives and money to project satellites and other objects into space. Yet we give no thought to what it will do to the universe!

"Fear inspired Columbus to seek a shorter way to the East so the stomachs of Europeans could be happy with spices.

"We hear of no ethical question on whether the natives on the moon (if any) would appreciate the earth's claiming it.

"Hallowe'en is our yearly Festival to honor FEAR. We camouflage in various costumes to evade the eyes of fear. Parents often join children in going from door to door to appeal for food they do not even need. We have the owl and the witch to sweep away superstition and cruelty."

From LITTLE LISTENING POST, Vol. 6, No. 1--

"A truism says that GREAT THINGS ARE SIMPLE. The AP says that 'government science leaders are warning that public disinterest and lack of money for research are endangering the U.S. Great scientist Oberth is declaring against rockets for space and in favor of some electrically propelled ships. Man is grappling with the greatest challenge of all time--trying to get off the planet. What is it, is not as complicated as it appears at Cape Canaveral."

There is talk of a United Nations University at either New York or Geneva where 10 or 15 thousand students from all over the world can pool their ideologies at Campus level and build contacts that would immresurably lessen world tensions.

From SPACECRAFTER, Vol. 3, No. 1

Los Angeles, Nov. 8--"A UCLA geophysicist has discovered a new land which lies thousands of feet beneath the ocean.

"Dr. John C. Harrison states that the land starts beneath the Gulf of California and goes down many thousands of feet, consisting mostly of valleys and ridges submerged beneath smooth layers of sand and mud, both of which have deposited thickly enough to smother the original features.

"Rock formations were mapped out by Dr. Harrison and Dr. Michael Caputo--Italy's University of Trieste--on the new land during their 2 months experience aboard the Horizon, Scripps Institute of Oceanography's 505-ton research vessel.

"The geophysicists have measured height and composition of ridges with a gravity meter, which indicates the pull of gravity on invisible rock formations.

"Accumulated data will take about a year to evaluate.

"The operation is taking place across the gulf between Baja, California, and the Mexican mainland.

- -

From LITTLE LISTENING POST, Vol. 6, No. 3:

"Solar aircraft has developed a fire-fighting missile which can reach the disaster scene 5 miles away in 1 minute, hover, spray a ton of extinguishing material."

- -

ROMAN SCRAPBOOK--

Mr. Railsbach, of Moline, Ill., came across this sentence in one of Obsequiens writings on ancient prophesies--"At sunset a circular object like a shield was seen to sweep across the sky from west to east." This was reported in 100 B.C. near Tarquinia, north of Rome.

- -

The lecture given by Dr. Wallace C. Halsey, Jan. 10, was very well attended. It was very well received, both spiritually and physically. We shall welcome Dr. Halsey and his lovely wife Tarna back here at any time in the future that they can come.

- -

Our tape librarian can furnish tapes for you. Many people are playing these tapes to groups in their homes, helping to spread the good work. Call or see Ken Priest, 3001 Norton, Independence, Mo., CL 4-5178.

See our book librarian Neal Pinkerton at the club lectures for your reading material. His address is 408 Greenway Terr., Kansas City, Mo., JA 3 2579.

- -

Return to:
Paul M. Wheeler
U.F.O. Study Club
1117 West Truman Road
Independence, Mo.

Vol. 2, No. 9 & 10   T H E S P A C E V I E W E R   JULIA BROGAN
March & April, 1960   UFO Study Club, Kansas City, Mo.   EDITOR
* *

COMING!   COMING!
GEORGE W. VAN TASSEL!
Thursday   Subject   Drexel Hall
April 14, 1960   "The Phenomena of the Times"   Linwood & Baltimore
8:00 P.M.   Kansas City, Mo.
Donations: $1.50 --- Juniors 50¢
BE THERE AND BRING ALL YOUR FRIENDS! MR. VAN TASSEL HAS A MESSAGE FOR ALL!

It is with the greatest of pleasure that the UFO Study Club of Kansas City announces George W. Van Tassel of Giant Rock, Calif., as our next speaker. He appears for the purpose of bringing his message to EVERYONE! His subject will be: "The Phenomena of the Times," and will include: Geophysical, Scientific, Economic, Religious and Political Aspects of the Spacecraft Appearing Around and Landing on the Earth.

Mr. Van Tassel has spent the past twelve years of his life in searching out the truths of the Saucer picture. He is the author of three books, "I Rode A Flying Saucer," and "Into This World and Out Again," and "The Council of Seven Lights." He is also the publisher of "Proceedings," a paper that carries much valuable information for all persons interested in the Saucer subject. It is also a branch of the Ministry of Universal Wisdom, Inc., a non-sectarian and non-profit organization.

Mr. Van Tassel is an ardent researcher and relates his many experiences with both space people and their craft. His information is rather unlimited, and he is a capable speaker and has sponsored the Giant Rock Space Convention during the past several years. This man is well worth hearing and is one of the very top men in the field. So come! Tell your friends! Your Club is expecting a turnout of record proportions! You are the one who is directly responsible for it! Talk it up and BE SURE TO COME YOURSELF AND BRING A CAR LOAD OF FRIENDS. Don't forget the date. Make this the most important date of the year up to now.

- - - - - - - - - - - - - -

MORE LECTURES COMING
MR. GEORGE KING OF LONDON, ENGLAND

Thursday Evening   Drexel Hall
April 21 at 8 P.M.   Donations $1.50 and 50¢ Juniors   Linwood & Baltimore

Mr. George King, leader of the Aetherius Society of London, England, will speak before our Club on Thursday evening, April 21, at 8:00 P.M. at Drexel Hall. As Mr. King describes his experience, he was first contacted by Space People in May 1954. Previous to that contact he had not heard of Flying Saucers except for occasional reports appearing in the English Press. Mr. King founded the Aetherius Society in London to propagate the great wisdom of these highly evolved beings from other planets. Come and hear of his many wonderful experiences. Tell everyone you see about this lecture.

- - - - - - - - - - - - - -

MR. RILEY CRABB OF B.S.R.A. TO GIVE A LECTURE

Mr. Riley Crabb, of Vista, California, will be here for a lecture to our Club on May 4th. He is the new director of Borderland Sciences Research Associates and is on tour, giving lectures in the mid-west. Keep this date in mind and we will be sending out more information about this lecture at a later date. Please keep this bulletin at hand so you can refer to these dates for our coming lectures. Mark these dates on your calendar so you won't forget them. They are important appointments!! These men are here for your pleasure and if you want to hear them you must make arrangements to do so!!!

- - - - - - - - - - - - - -

"COLLEGE OF KNOWLEDGE" NEWS LETTER FROM THE HALSEY'S--Been receiving them since they went back west. They have meetings at their place on Wednesday, Friday and Saturday evenings and Sunday afternoons, 731 So. Serrano, Los Angeles 5, California. Their News Letter is really newsy, anyone interested can write them about it.

From "My Weekly Reader", the Junior newspaper for schools: "MOON RELAY. The Navy has set up a communication system by way of the moon. The system links Maryland and Hawaii. The first message was sent a few weeks ago. It was a radiophotograph spelling out the words, "Moon relay." The moon-relay system has one big advantage over present radio links. It will not be bothered by noise interferences or blackouts. The main disadvantage is that radio contact can be made only when the moon is above the horizon at both Maryland and Hawaii."

"Every thought sent forth is a never ending vibration winging its way across the universe to bring us back just what we sent forth. We CAN control the vibrations that emanate from US--and WE CAN hereby control OUR destinies."

"INTERSTELLAR LISTENING MAY PROVE LUCRETIUS RIGHT 20 CENTURIES AGO"--In 65 B.C. a Roman named Lucretius shocked his followers with a fantastic thought:"All this visible universe is not unique in nature, and we must believe that there are, in other regions of space, other worlds, other beings and other men."....In 1960 A.D.--sometime next month (March) two Americans, at work in a West Virginia valley, will flick a switch and patiently attempt to prove that Lucretius was right. As casually as a neighbor phoning to ask whether she can borrow a cup of sugar, they'll be inquiring:"Are you there, Tau Ceti?" And saying hopefully: "Come in, Epsilon Eridani!"...They'll be banking on the possibility that these two neighbors, a mere 66,000,000,000,000 miles away, will, at the precise moment W. Virginia is listening, be speaking to us...In what language? Possibly in mathematics. Or chemistry. Fantastic? It certainly is. But this is the SPACE AGE. And more rapidly than anyone had dreamed possible, the world of Buck Rogers and Jules Verne is catching up with reality...From Kansas City Star, Feb.27.

Also from the Kansas City Paper comes these items:--Alamogordo, N.M.,March 12. (AP) An official of an organization dedicated to the study of unidentified flying objects (UFO) said today the group has physical evidence of the existence of such phenomena. And a challenge was issued to the U. S. Air Force to try to refute the evidence. The challenge came in a letter from Mrs. Coral E. Lorenzen of Alamogordo, who is an international director of the Aerial Phenomena Research Organization. Mrs. Lorenzen said today A.P.R.O. has in its possession two pieces of material found after what she termed "an extraterrestrial vehicle...met with disaster in the earth's atmosphere." Mrs. Lorenzen's letter was sent to Major Lawrence J. Tacker of the office of public information in Washington.

Major Keyhoe in the news again..."Hide Facts on Flying Saucer"..March 19,Washington, D.C...Maj. Donald E. Keyhoe, retired, director of N.I.C.A.P. accuses air force of not giving correct story in one instance of a mysterious round flying object sighted at Redmond, Oregon, September 24, 1959. He says, "The Air Force was fully aware that its own and the FAA evidence proved this was some unknown machine under intelligent control. We believe that the public interest is best served by honest official statements disclosing the full details in all U.F.O. cases investigated by the U.S. Air Force, and that concealing the facts will only arouse public suspicion and harm."

After a few items like these in the Kansas City papers we find this editorial: "THE FLYING SAUCERS ARE BACK"-March 25....Anyone who believed (or hoped) that the flying saucer issue had been dropped now may be disappointed. It's popped back into the news. Not only do people keep seeing strange flying things, the Air Force has been charged anew with concealing saucer facts. For years, the air arm has conducted periodic investigations of unidentified flying objects. Repeatedly, the service has concluded that virtually all U.F.O.'s can be attributed to natural phenomena. Air officials say there never has been evidence to confirm ideas that U.F.O.'s may be interplanetary space-ships...But recently Donald Keyhoe, director of a nongovernment committee to investigate saucer-type things in the sky, accused the Air Force of covering up the facts. Keyhoe, a retired Marine officer, has written books and articles to present the view that saucers really are vehicles manned by forces from Venus, Mars, or somewhere else out there....So, here we go again!!

From LLP, Washington, D.C.: EXTRA! HOLD EVERYTHING! WE HAVE SEEN THE REAL McCOY! It is a published document that seems due to change the status of something dear to the heart of many a Researcher. It was published in an obscure place and its coverage very limited. Whether or not someone "Intentionally" 'left the back door open' is not known - since SOME things may best come out gradually. That's why we must delay giving you DETAILS right now. However, you will unquestionably be hearing a lot about it before long. That's all we can tell you at this time. "A WORTHY STATEMENT," say the comments, "BUT ABOUT TEN YEARS LATE!"

MAN REACHES EVER FARTHER OUT!...WHO OWNS THE CLOUDS?--This may soon become a legal question. A N.Y. firm plans to use them as "billboards", A "Skyjector" mounted on a 4-ton truck will cast messages on them readable 10 miles away; will the very clouds then howl to us about what beer to drink! What may this mean, for good or bad? Will commercialism gobble up the beauties of our skies and clouds - against which we love to write the private thoughts of our own inner communing?

THE PASSING SCENE:"Every day 100,000 Human Beings finish their Earthly Span and "pass off" into the Vast BEYOND! "Where are they? Where do they go?... In Singapore is the "strangest street in the world"-the STREET OF THE DYING, niches where Chinese go to die - Temple, Casket Mfgs., Undertakers all nearby, often Holy Men attend the Dying and by SUGGESTION usher them consciously into "liberation" till 'silver cord' is severed...There is more and more talk of BY-PASSING DEATH, that DEATH means DEFEAT!, it is an 'ENEMY' "the LAST ENEMY that SHALL BE OVERCOME"; continued interest in Annalee Skarin, said to have TRANSMUTED yet appears in 3-D at will, then VANISHES! Many feel we may be nearing the time when 'Ye shall be changed in the twinkling of an eye, SOME NEW CONCEPT SEEMS TO BE COMING IN, WATCH: "And there shall be no more death...for the former things are passed away" St. John. The CONCEPT (conception) MUST come first--WE ARE IN THE AGE OF MARVELS!! "The Law of the Spirit of Life hath made me FREE from the law of sin and DEATH",--one group has out stickers - "IMMORTALITY NOW."

MANY SAUCERS STILL DO "NAME-CALLING" AMONG THEMSELVES - a trait of the spiritually immature -- LET'S BATTLE PRINCIPLES, NOT PERSONALITIES! - Ed.

SOMEONE HAS SAID "ALL THINGS ARE BORN OF LONELINESS."

We certainly appreciate the NEWS received in the LLP. We think it one of the finest publications in the field.

Another one is the Cosmic Digest published and edited by our own member Dwight Bockman under the name of Cosmic Press, Box 316, Independence, Mo. The second edition is just off the press.

From THIS WEEK magazine of March 20 comes another article by Dr. Werner Von Braun...
WHY SHOULD AMERICA CONQUER SPACE?...Excerpts from this are: When we speak of the "Conquest of Space" we had better clarify that term right at the outset. For one thing, we do not mean conquest in the sense of beating little green men into submission and staking out a nationalistic claim on the Universe. Also, space is a pretty big place--they say it is even bigger than Texas and Alaska thrown together. Not even the boldest science fiction writer would ever dream of earth men exploring all the space from here to infinity. When we speak of conquest of space we mean no more than visits to a few of our close celestial neighbors. Nevertheless, some of these neighboring stars may be just as intriguing and just as full of mysteries as our own little planet which until the dawn of the Space Age we called The World...Why must we take up this challenge? Why must we conquer space now that we have the technical ability to do it? Dr. James R. Killian, the President's former Scientific Advisor, gave us the main reason"the compelling urge to explore the unknown."...Just plain curiosity has always been a far more effective mainspring for research and exploration than hope for economic returns. ...Space lies out there like a vast, unexplored ocean--accessible to all nations large or small, a challenge for anyone with sailor's blood in his veins. Now that for the first time in history man is about ready and able to build ships which can penetrate that ocean, there can be no question that some men will take up the challenge. Some of them will make great discoveries out there, and some of these discoveries will greatly affect the course of history on our home planet. Shall we exclude ourselves from this contest because we prefer to "devote our riches to luxury?"...We have just opened the door into the limitless reaches of the Universe and we can see just far enough ahead to know that man is at the threshold of a momentous area. Here is opportunity, challenge, adventure so tremendous as to exceed anything which has bone before

...It is impossible to predict the nature of all these discoveries: their cumulative effect will be tantamount to a scientific revolution. But it will also be a revolution of human perspective, and here may be space flight's most far-reaching pay off. We need not fear that future space explorers on their heaven-storming journeys will lose their humility. The heavens will surround them as an eternal reminder that there is a force greater than the thrust of their rocket ships, a spirit greater than the cold logic of their computers, a power greater than that of their own nation.

"Every man should live because upon his shoulders rests a divine responsibility. It has been said by many: "This old world owes me a living." That is not true. This world owes nothing to any of us. We have plundered her, robbed her, torn her jewels from her brow, bared her nakedness, feasted upon the very life of her, gouged into her very heart and at the same time continually cursed her. No man has the right to live upon this earth who does not contribute something of value in return--buildings--bridges--highways--art--melody or great understanding and kindness, for every man was created to be a messenger of light and crowned with a high destiny."('Ye Are Gods' by Annalee Skarin)

What you don't know you can always learn....Men who do things that count never stop to count them....Not what you do, but how you do it.

A CHALLENGE TO SPIRITUAL LEADERS!! Excerpts from this pamphlet by George Adamski:"The reality of these ships from other planets BELONG IN THE REALM OF THE COSMOS. Therefore those who could best bring forth the truth to the whole of mankind and establish friendly relations between the visitors and ourselves, would be THE GREAT RELIGIONS OF THE WORLD, united in at least this one purpose. Such union would inevitably lead to further unity in which the hairs of difference in creed and dogma would no longer seem worth splitting. I believe this whole phenomena has reached a point where it should be recognized as a fulfillment of long cherished dreams and hopes, whereby man once again will understand his relationship to the Cosmos itself."

Remember our tape Librarian, if you want to borrow tapes for playing to groups in your home, call or see Ken Priest, 3001 Norton, Independence, Mo.

Mr. A. Neal Pinkerton has a large selection of books in the Club library and they are always on display at our meetings.

Small minds discuss persons---Average minds discuss events---Great minds discuss ideas!! Which class are we in?

Remember these dates: April 14th--Van Tassel. April 21st--George King. May 4th--Riley Crabb.

Return to
Paul M. Wheeler
U.F.O. Study Club
1117 W. Truman Rd.
Independence, Mo.

```
* * * * * * * * * * * * * * * * * * * * * * * * * * * * * * * * * * * * * * *
* Vol. 3 No. 2        T H E  S P A C E V I E W E R           Thelma Olson   *
* January, 1961         U. F. O. Study Club of Kansas City, Mo.    Editor   *
*              "A down-to-earth study of things up in the sky."             *
* * * * * * * * * * * * * * * * * * * * * * * * * * * * * * * * * * * * * * *
```

| Non-Profit | Non-Political | Non-Sectarian |

SPECIAL BULLETIN!   COMING -- JANUARY 8   DON'T MISS IT!

ANNOUNCING DR. WALLACE C. HALSEY
Will Lecture
SUNDAY AFTERNOON, JANUARY 8, 1961
Drexel Hall, Linwood and Baltimore
Time 3:00 P.M.

SUBJECT: "HUMMING IN THE UNIVERSE"

Dr. Wallace C. Halsey, D. D., L. L. D., professional engineer, lecturer, scholar and minister, president of Christ Brotherhood Evangelistic Association, College of Knowledge, of Logan, Utah, will give a lecture at Drexel Hall, corner Linwood and Baltimore Streets (one block west of Main), Kansas City, Missouri.

The lecture is scheduled for Sunday afternoon at 3:00 o'clock, January 8, 1961. Dr. Halsey's subject will be: "Humming in the Universe". It is reported he has a lot of wonderful new information to present at this time that should be of interest to people of all walks of life.

Dr. Halsey's experiences consist of a wide range of subjects, including the coming of Space Ships in our skies and their purpose in being here; the story of creation; our solar system and balance; the Tower of Babel; the twelve planets of our solar system; functions of the Pyramids; the California pyramid; Infinite light; positive and negative light; "squaring" the body; the pineal gland; third eye development; life on Saturn; the center of the earth; the effects of the destruction of the planet Lucifer; the unnatural crust of the surface of the earth; differences in the construction of space ships of Mars, Venus and Saturn; the transistor beam, and others.

Dr. Halsey has traveled far and wide and is thoroughly qualified to speak on this most timely subject. The public is urged to attend this lecture and become informed concerning this interesting phenomena of our time. Tell your friends and bring a carload with you.

Donations: Adults, $1.50 - - Juniors, 50¢

Please post this bulletin.

A veritable cornucopia of news and information in the field of UFOlogy is the LITTLE LISTENING POST (LLP) at WASHINGTON, D.C. It contains several pages of straight reading material, no advertisements, and is well worth the price of $3.00 for six issues. It is published "every few weeks", as the editor says. For further information or a subscription write to the editor of the LLP at 4811 Illinois Avenue, Washington, D.C.

```
* * * * * * * * * * * * * * * * * * * * * * * * * * * * * * * * * * * * * * *
*  SEASON'S GREETINGS TO ALL OF YOU:                                        *
*                                                                           *
*  Words do not express the appreciation for our many friends and the love in our *
*  hearts for each one. At this most lovely season of the year we wish for you *
*  God's richest blessings, and may His peace abide with you always!        *
*                                                                           *
*                                       Paul and Luella Wheeler and         *
*                                       Members of the Executive Board      *
* * * * * * * * * * * * * * * * * * * * * * * * * * * * * * * * * * * * * * *
```

MYSTERIOUS GLOW IN SKY

An Associated Press release in papers on Thanksgiving Day told of a mysterious glow in the sky just around dawn the day before and seen over a vast Midwest and Eastern area of the nation. The light was described as bigger than the moon and seemingly trailing smoke or a comet-like tail.

Various experts over the area were said to have attributed the glow to various causes: Dropping of tinfoil chaff at high altitude by jet aircraft in radar jamming exercises near Detroit; a huge weather balloon sent up at 4:00 A. M. EST over Sioux Falls, S. D.,; Tiros II sent up at Cape Canaveral, Fla.; phenomena in the skies caused by the sun's rays; a rocket; a flying saucer.

Did all these things happen simultaneously? Was one cause responsible for this big glow? Does anyone know for certain? We're curious.

THE CLUB LIBRARY

The Club has a growing library of books and magazines on UFO's, sightings, "flying saucers" through the ages, and related material, as well as some books of fiction not related to UFO's.

(continued over)

CLUB LIBRARY (Cont)

Much credit should be given to A. Neal Pinkerton for his work as book librarian. He has selected many of the books in the library. Other books have been donated by club members.

Mr. Pinkerton has worked out a simple but quite effective system of cataloging and indexing the books, as well as a card control system. The books are always at the library counter during each lecture meeting.

Those wishing to borrow books are required to pay a deposit, with club members being entitled to a reduced deposit price. Patrons are allowed to keep books for four weeks. Those finding themselves unable to return the books personally may mail them to Mr. Pinkerton, Box 412, Main Post Office, Kansas City, Mo. If the package is marked LIBRARY MATERIAL the mailing rate is much lower than the regular parcel post rate.

WILLIAMSON SPEAKS AT NOVEMBER MEETING

In his address on Tuesday night, Nov. 29, at Drexel Hall, Dr. George Hunt Williamson kept his audience keenly interested as he spoke on the "Footprints of Prophecy." As an introduction to his lecture, Dr. Williamson gave the highlights of his growing interest in space ships following the Kenneth Arnold incident in 1947. This interest developed into his radio contacts with the intelligences operating the UFO's, or space craft, and finally to a meeting between Williamson and George Adamski for the purpose of seeing a UFO at close range in a vicinity where others had seen such crafts. The effort was successful. The meeting was made in November, 1952, and although only Adamski made the actual contact, Dr. Williamson took pictures of the locale after the craft took off into the air. He also took snapshots of the footprints of the space man and made some plaster casts of the footprints which enabled him to make drawings of the symbols in the footprints. Dr. Williamson believes the symbols were on an outer layer of material attached to the sandal soles for the sole purpose of leaving a message to earth people.

Dr. Williamson used slides to illustrate his lecture in which he gave his interpretation of the symbols in the footprints, showing how the symbols depicted man's past, present and future on earth.

As an anthropologist, Dr. Williamson has gathered a vast collection of legends and folk lore from various tribes of Indians, both in North and South America. Nearly all North American tribes, he said, have stories of "heavenly visitors" who came to bring help to their people. These stories are all very similar to each other and are almost identical to stories of actual contacts and sightings of "flying saucers" by people today. One message given to Williamson and his friends was that all through history the UFO's have always appeared during times of great crisis.

Dr. Williamson was accompanied by his assistant, Greg Beamer.

UNSCHEDULED MEETING HELD IN DECEMBER

Major Wayne S. Aho arrived here December first for a lecture that evening. With very short notice beforehand, it was impossible to send out announcements and also impossible to secure Drexel Hall. The meeting was held in Watson Memorial Church in Independence, as announced from the platform at the Williamson lecture. A fair-sized group attended.

Major Aho spoke at length on the spiritual aspects of UFOlogy, relating his own spiritual experience of last winter. Many favorable comments were made on the lecture.

By recent action of the Executive Board, the tape librarian, Ken Priest, is the only one authorized to dispense tapes of lectures to other organizations. Only those holding membership in the U.F.O. Study Club of Kansas City are entitled to make tapes of lectures; others must have special permission from the club president, Paul Wheeler.

A new product now being offered is being vouched for enthusiastically by those in this community who have given it a fair trial. It is called Mineralife, is a natural mineral food and may be secured locally from both Paul Wheeler and Ken Priest.

Paul M. Wheeler
1117 W. Truman Road
Independence, Mo.